THE ILLUSTRATED

WORLD ATLAS

DR. ALISDAIR ROGERS

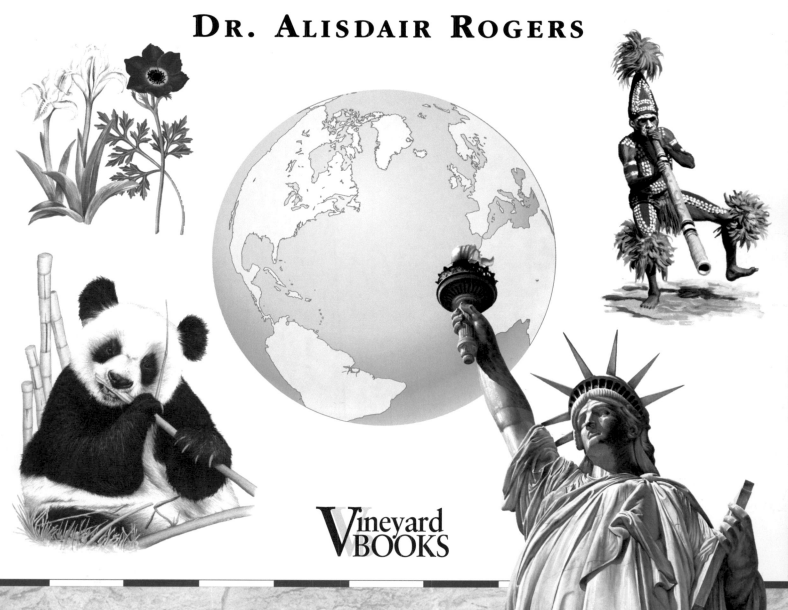

Vineyard
BOOKS

Planned and produced by:
Andromeda Oxford Limited
11-13 The Vineyard
Abingdon
Oxon OX14 3PX
England

Published in 1998 by:
Andromeda Oxford Limited
11-13 The Vineyard
Abingdon
Oxon OX14 3PX
England

Designed by: Sally Boothroyd, Nick Leggett
Edited by: Neil Morris, Vicky Egan
Maps by: Julian Baker
Illustrations by: John Downes, Stuart Lafford, Stephen Lings, Jane Pickering, Chris Rothero, Eric Rowe, Sarah Smith (Linden Artists); Mike Bell (Specs Art); Tim Haywood

ISBN 1-86199-037-5
Printed and bound by
Poligrafici Calderara S.p.A,
Bologna, Italy.

PICTURE CREDITS
Abbreviations
HL–The Hutchison Library
ISI–Chris Fairclough at Image Select International
LF–Life File Photographic Library
MP–Magnum Photos
NHPA–Natural History Photographic Agency
RHPL–Robert Harding Picture Library
SAP–South American Pictures

7tr John Shaw/NHPA; 7bl Robert Francis/HL; 7br Jeremy Horner/Panos Pictures; 10t Stuart Franklin/MP; 10bl ISI; 10br Nik Wheeler/RHPL; 11t, 11b ISI; 12t ISI; 12c Ralph Clevenger/ RHPL; 13t Trevor Page/HL; 13c ISI; 13bl Ralph Clevenger/RHPL; 14cl ISI; 14b Ernst Haas/MP; 15tl Adam Woolfitt/RHPL; 15tr Simon Harris/RHPL; 15b, 16t ISI; 16cl Simon Harris/RHPL; 17t ISI; 17cr T. Kitchen and V. Hurst/NHPA; 18t ISI; 18b The Walt Disney Company, 1996; 19tl ISI; 19tr The Stock Market; 19br Ford Motor Company; 20bl Robert Frerck/RHPL; 20br Thomas Hoepker/MP; 21d Philip Wolmuth/HL; 21tr Abbas/MP; 22tr RHPL; 23t Chris Sharp/ SAP; 23cr Robert Cundy/RHPL; 23bl J. Henderson/HL; 24cl Nancy Durrell McKenna/HL; 24bl, 25tl Tony Morrison/SAP; 25cr Michael Nichols/MP; 25bl Griffiths/MP; 26t ISI; 26cl HL; 26cr Tony Morrison/SAP; 27b

ISI; 28cl, 28cr Tony Morrison/ SAP; 28-29 Stuart Franklin/MP; 29cl Stephanie Maze/Woodfin Camp and Associates; 29cr Robert Francis/SAP; 30t Adam Woolfitt/RHPL; 30cl, 30bl, 30br ISI; 31t Fraser Ralston/LF; 31b ISI; 32t IKEA; 32b David Woodfall/NHPA; 33cl Harry Gruyaert/MP; 33br B. and C. Alexander/NHPA; 34tr ISI; 34cl The Stock Market; 34br Roy Rainford/RHPL; 35t RHPL; 35cr Simon Harris/RHPL; 36tr Bojan Brecelj/Still Pictures; 36br Eric Soder/NHPA; 37bl E.A. Janes/ NHPA; 38tr K. Gillham/RHPL; 38cr Fred Mayer/MP; 38bl ISI; 39tl Harry Gruyaert/MP; 39cr, 40t ISI; 40cl Fred Mayer/MP; 40bl Graham Burns/LF; 41t NASA/Science Photo Library; 41cr Christopher Rennie/RHPL; 41bl Ellen Rooney/RHPL; 42t Bruno Barbey/MP; 42cl V. Ivleva/HL; 42-43 Andrey Zvoznikov/HL; 43br John G. Egan/HL; 44tr ISI; 44c Matthew Kneale; 44bl HL; 44br, 45tl Abbas/MP; 45tr E. Simanor/ RHPL; 46c Sassoon/RHPL; 46bl RHPL; 47tl Robin Constable/ HL; 47br, 48t, 48cl, 48cr, 48b, 49tl, 49tr, 50tr ISI; 50bl Martin Harvey/NHPA; 51t, 51cr ISI; 52t, 52cl RHPL; 52b Peter Barker/Panos Pictures; 52-53 Gina Green/LF; 53t ISI; 53b Raghu Rai/MP; 54cl Gavin Hellier/RHPL; 54bl RHPL; 54br, 55tl ISI; 55tr Gavin Hellier/ RHPL; 55b Richard Powers/LF;

56cl ISI; 56-57 Peter Marlow/ MP; 57tl Master Printers' Association; 57cr ISI; 57br Images Colour Library; 58t R. Ian Lloyd/HL; 58c ISI; 58bl Rainbird/ RHPL; 59tr G. Pinkhassov/MP; 59bl, 60t, 60cl ISI; 60bl John Hatt/HL; 61t ISI; 61cl Chris Stowers/Panos Pictures; 60-61 Charles Moore/Black Star/ Colorific; 62t RHPL; 62cl Gavin Hellier/RHPL; 62cr ISI; 62b Marc Riboud/MP; 63t Liaison/Frank Spooner Pictures; 63c ISI; 63cr Kaku Kurita/ Gamma Press/Frank Spooner Pictures; 64cl ISI; 64c Ian Murphy/Tony Stone Images; 64bl James Martin/Tony Stone Images; 65tr ISI; 65c Hilarie Kavanagh/ Tony Stone Images; 65b A. Perrier/ RHPL; 67t John Shaw/ NHPA; 68tr Sarah Errington/ HL; 68cl HL; 68bl Anthony Bannister/NHPA; 68-69 Liba Taylor/HL; 69tl The Stock Market; 69bl PowerStock Photo Library; 69br H. Rogers/ TRIP; 70t Bill Ross/West Light/RHPL; 70bl C. Bowman/RHPL; 70br ISI; 71t Burt Glinn/MP; 71c David Cannon/Allsport; 71b ISI; 73tr Nicola Wells/LF; 74t James Strachan/RHPL; 74cl Aubrey J. Slaughter/LF; 74bl P. Zachmann/ MP; 74br Catrina Thompson/LF; 75t RHPL; 75bl ISI; 75br Peter Marlow/MP; 76cl RHPL; 76br The Stock Market; 77c Sassoon/ RHPL; 77cr Geoff Renner/ RHPL; 77bl Dr. David Millar/ Science Photo Library.

Contents

How to use this atlas

This atlas divides the world up into 15 regions. Some of the regions, like Canada, are made up of just one country. But most of them, like Africa, have lots of countries. On the map on the right, each region is shown in a different colour so that you can see at a glance which countries are in each region. Some small islands not shown on the regional maps in the atlas have also been named here. If you want to find a particular country, city, river, mountain or island on one of the maps in this atlas, first look up the name of the place in the gazetteer and index at the back of the book. Next to the name of the place you will see a page number and a grid reference of letters and numbers. Turn to the right page, and then use the grid at the edges of the pages to find the place on the map. (On this page, Mexico's grid reference is F8.)

MAPPING THE WORLD

The Earth is a round planet, which makes it very difficult to show on the flat pages of an atlas. To overcome this problem, map-makers cut the world up into segments, rather like peeling an orange, and lay the segments out flat. The result is a flat map of the round Earth, like the one above.

CARIBBEAN ISLANDS
(dependencies in *italics*)
1. *TURKS & CAICOS ISLANDS (UK)*
2. *CAYMAN ISLANDS (UK)*
3. HAITI
4. JAMAICA
5. *PUERTO RICO (US)*
6. *VIRGIN ISLANDS (US/UK)*
7. *ANGUILLA (UK)*
8. ST KITTS & NEVIS
9. ANTIGUA & BARBUDA
10. *GUADELOUPE (FR)*
11. *MONTSERRAT (UK)*
12. DOMINICA
13. *MARTINIQUE (FR)*
14. ST LUCIA
15. ST VINCENT & THE GRENADINES
16. GRENADA
17. BARBADOS
18. TRINIDAD & TOBAGO
19. *ARUBA (NETH)*
20. *NETHERLANDS ANTILLES (NETH)*

User's Guide

Locator globes show the position of each region in the world.

Data files give essential facts and figures, including population and land area of the region.

The **compass** points to north, and the scale bar below shows distance in kilometres and miles.

National flags of all independent countries in the region are shown at the top of the pages, together with land area and population of each country.

BRUNEI
Area: 5,765 sq km
Population: 307,000

N

Kilometres
0   1000   2000   3000

0   1000   2000
Miles

Data file

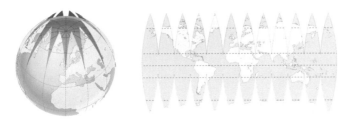

3,859,991 sq km/1,490,354 sq mi
478 million
31
Ukraine (603,700 sq km/233,100 sq mi)
Vatican City (0.44 sq km/0.17 sq mi)
190,000)
Spain (3 million)

Area
Population
countries

ARCTIC OCEAN

ARCTIC OCEAN

LAND

FAEROE
ISLANDS
(DENMARK)

IRELAND

NORWAY
SWEDEN
FINLAND

DENMARK
ESTONIA
LATVIA

UNITED
KINGDOM

21 22
BELARUS

24 23
POLAND

26
UKRAINE

RUSSIA

KAZAKHSTAN

MONGOLIA

25
FRANCE
33 32 28 31
35 36 30
34 SAN
MARINO
ITALY 40
GREECE
BULGARIA
GEORGIA
AZERBAIJAN
UZBEKISTAN

KYRGYZSTAN
TAJIKISTAN

CHINA

NORTH
KOREA
SOUTH
KOREA
JAPAN

N

MADEIRA
(PORT)

CANARY
ISLANDS
(ITALY)

PORTUGAL
SPAIN

MOROCCO

ARMENIA
TURKEY

CYPRUS
SYRIA
LEBANON
ISRAEL
IRAQ
IRAN
AFGHANI-
STAN

JORDAN
KUWAIT
BAHRAIN
QATAR

PAKISTAN

NEPAL
BHUTAN

PACIFIC
OCEAN

Kilometres

0   1000   2000   3000

0   1000   2000

Miles

WESTERN
SAHARA

ALGERIA
LIBYA
EGYPT
SAUDI
ARABIA

UNITED
ARAB
EMIRATES
OMAN
YEMEN

BANGLADESH

INDIA

MYANMAR

TAIWAN

MAURITANIA
MALI
NIGER
CHAD
SUDAN
ERITREA
DJIBOUTI

LACCADIVE IS.
(INDIA)

ANDAMAN IS.
(INDIA)

NICOBAR IS.
(INDIA)

THAILAND
VIETNAM

LAOS

NORTHERN
MARIANA IS.
(USA)

WAKE
ISLAND
(USA)

MARSHALL IS.

SENEGAL
BURKINA
FASO
NIGERIA

IVORY
COAST
SIERRA
LEONE
LIBERIA
GHANA TOGO
BENIN
CAMEROON
SAO TOME & PRINCIPE
EQUATORIAL
GUINEA

CENTRAL
AFRICAN
REPUBLIC
UGANDA

ETHIOPIA

SOMALIA

MALDIVES

SRI
LANKA

CAMBODIA

PHILIPPINES

BRUNEI
MALAYSIA

GUAM (USA)

PALAU

MICRONESIA

ASCENSION
ISLAND
(UK)

GABON
CONGO
CABINDA
(ANGOLA)

DEMOCRATIC
REPUBLIC
OF
CONGO
RWANDA
BURUNDI
KENYA

TANZANIA

SEYCHELLES
COMOROS
MAYOTTE
(FR)

SINGAPORE

INDIAN
OCEAN

INDONESIA

NEW GUINEA
PAPUA
NEW
GUINEA

NAURU

SOLOMON
IS.

KIRIBATI

TUVALU

TOKELAU
(NZ)

ST HELENA
(UK)

ANGOLA
ZAMBIA
MALAWI

NAMIBIA
ZIMBABWE
BOTSWANA

MADAGASCAR
MAURITIUS

RÉUNION
(FR)

CORAL
SEA IS.

WALLIS &
FUTUNA
(FR)

VANUATU

SAMOA
FIJI

AMERICAN
SAMOA
(USA)

TONGA

COOK
IS.
(NZ)

ATLANTIC
OCEAN

MOZAMBIQUE

SWAZILAND
SOUTH
AFRICA
LESOTHO

NEW CALEDONIA (FR)

AUSTRALIA

TRISTAN DA
CUNHA
(UK)

TASMANIA

NEW
ZEALAND

EUROPEAN COUNTRIES	25 LUXEMBOURG	30 ROMANIA	36 CROATIA
21 RUSSIA	26 GERMANY	31 HUNGARY	37 BOSNIA-HERZEGOVINA
22 LITHUANIA	27 CZECH REPUBLIC	32 AUSTRIA	38 YUGOSLAVIA
23 NETHERLANDS	28 SLOVAKIA	33 SWITZERLAND	39 MACEDONIA
24 BELGIUM	29 MOLDOVA	34 ANDORRA	40 ALBANIA
		35 SLOVENIA	

ANTARCTICA

CHINA'S FARMING REGIONS

Only one-tenth of China's land area is suitable for cultivation. Half of this is given over to paddy fields or irrigated for other crops such as cabbages and carrots. Rice, the main crop, is grown mainly in the south. Almost one-third of China is used for herding livestock, raised mainly for meat.

Sugar cane, mandarins and pineapples grow in warm Guanxi province.

Guangdong is an important area for cabbages and carrots.

Melons and other fruit are grown in oases in the western deserts.

Yaks are raised on the high plateau of Tibet.

Forest

Herding

Captions give information about special places and areas within a large region.

Special feature maps show particular aspects of a region, such as its farming or industry.

Letters, numbers and a blue-and-white border form a grid that cross-references with the gazetteer and index to give map locations.

M

N

23

MAP KEY

■ Paris	Country capital
● Qamdo	City
Quebec ✲	Canadian province and US state capitals
	Country border
	Disputed country border
	River
Mt Everest	Mountain
PUERTO RICO (USA)	Dependency (controlling country in brackets)

Our planet in space

The universe contains millions of galaxies, and each one — even the smallest — is made up of millions of stars. One of those millions of stars, in the galaxy called the Milky Way, is our own Sun. All life on Earth depends on the Sun's energy, which gives humans, animals and plants light and warmth. The Earth travels around the Sun. It takes a year for it to go round it once; and because the Earth is tilted, we have seasons. For example, for the part of the year that the north is nearer the Sun than the south, we have northern summers and southern winters. The Earth also spins as it travels, giving us night and day.

OUR GALAXY

Astronomers think that there are about 100,000 million galaxies in the universe. Our galaxy, the Milky Way (left), is just one of them. It is spiral shaped, with curved "arms", and is made up of about 100,000 million stars! Our Sun is a star on one of its arms. On clear nights, you can see some of the stars in the Milky Way forming a bright band of "milky-coloured" light across the sky.

THE SOLAR SYSTEM

The Earth is one of nine planets that travel around the star which we call the Sun. These nine planets, together with their moons and the Sun, make up the solar system. Mercury (1, above) is the closest planet to the Sun, followed by Venus (2), Earth (3), Mars (4), Jupiter (5), Saturn (6), Uranus (7), Neptune (8) and Pluto(9). Pluto is the smallest planet and is furthest from the Sun.

INSIDE THE EARTH

The Earth is like a giant ball made up of different layers. The outer layer is called the Earth's crust. All the continents and the oceans shown on the maps in this atlas lie on the Earth's crust. Movements of huge pieces of the crust, called plates, cause earthquakes. Below the crust is the mantle. Sometimes the mantle's molten rock, called magma, breaks through cracks in the crust and forms volcanoes. Deeper down, the Earth's core is made up of two parts: a liquid outer core and a solid inner core.

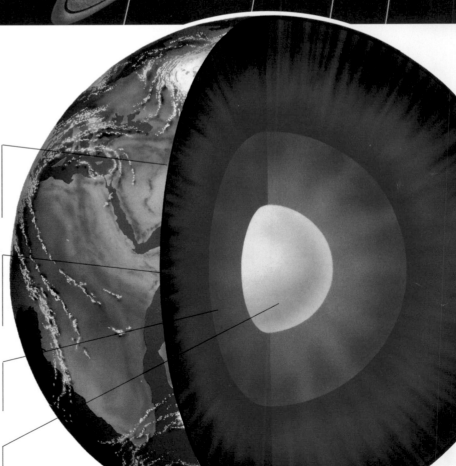

The crust, the Earth's hard outer layer, is up to 50 km (31 mi) thick under the oceans and continents.

The mantle goes down to a depth of 2,900 km (1,800 mi). In some places the hot rocks move very slowly.

The outer core is a very hot, thick liquid made of iron and nickel.

The inner core is under such pressure that it is solid mass.

Climate and vegetation

The climate — or typical weather conditions — of a region depends on its location. Regions close to the equator are hottest, and those nearest the poles are coldest. In between there are temperate, or mild, regions. How high a place is above sea level, and how near it is to a coast, also affect its climate. Coastal areas tend to have warmer winters and cooler summers than inland areas. The climate of a place has a major influence on its vegetation, or plant life.

TEMPERATE FOREST

This type of mild-weather forest occurs in North America, Europe and the far east of Asia. It is made up mainly of broadleaf, "deciduous" trees, which means they shed their leaves in winter. Before they drop, the autumn leaves turn brilliant shades of red and yellow. These temperate forest trees (above) are in the Great Smoky Mountains National Park, Tennessee, USA.

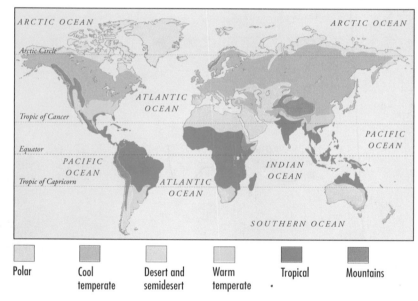

Polar | Cool temperate | Desert and semidesert | Warm temperate | Tropical | Mountains

LANDSCAPES AND CLIMATE

In the tropics — the area between the Tropic of Cancer and the Tropic of Capricorn — there is dense tropical forest, rainfall is over 2,000 mm (80 in) a year and temperatures average 25° C (77° F). Deserts cover one-seventh of the Earth; here it can be over 37° C (100° F) by day, but below freezing at night. In the Arctic polar region there is a treeless tundra landscape of low-growing plants and mosses around the edge of the ice sheets. Farther south, in the cool temperate region, there are vast bands of coniferous forest. These give way to deciduous forest and grassland in the warm temperate region.

TROPICAL RAINFOREST

In tropical regions near the equator, the climate is hot and wet all year round. These conditions create habitats that support more kinds of plants and animals than anywhere else. Tropical rainforests are found in Central and South America, Africa, South East Asia and northern Australia. The trees often support climbing plants, and are home to colourful birds, monkeys and other animals (right). Unfortunately, huge areas of rainforest are being cut down to provide people with fuelwood and to create farmland. Conservationists worldwide are trying hard to stop the destruction of these important habitats.

DRY SOUTH AMERICA

The Atacama Desert (above), in Chile, is probably the driest place on Earth. A squall of rain may strike small parts of it several times in a hundred years!

WET SOUTH AMERICA

Tutunendo, in Colombia (above), lies about 3,000 km (1,850 mi) north of the dry Atacama Desert. It is one of the wettest places in the world!

The world's top five

The world is full of amazing natural and human-made wonders, from mighty rivers that cross continents to cities with more people than some countries. All the world's highest mountains are in the same mountain range: the Himalayas, between China and Pakistan, India, Nepal and Bhutan. But most of the rest of the record features — the largest lakes and islands, for example — are spread out across the world. The world's "top fives" are all shown on the map opposite.

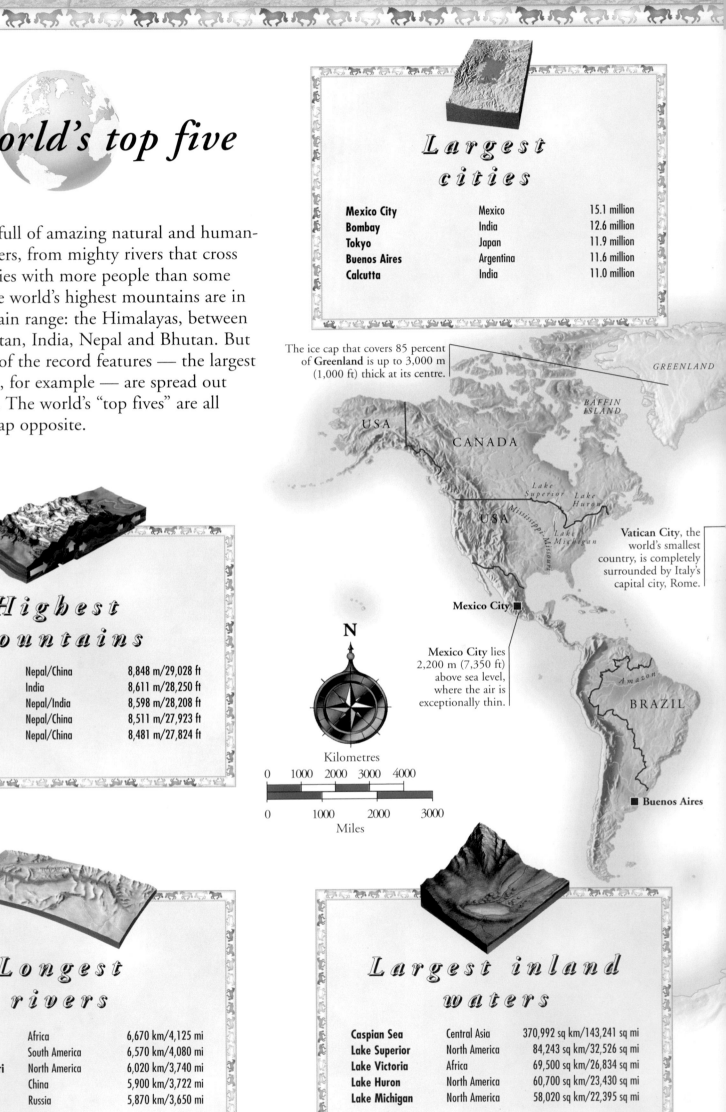

Largest cities

Mexico City	Mexico	15.1 million
Bombay	India	12.6 million
Tokyo	Japan	11.9 million
Buenos Aires	Argentina	11.6 million
Calcutta	India	11.0 million

The ice cap that covers 85 percent of **Greenland** is up to 3,000 m (1,000 ft) thick at its centre.

GREENLAND

BAFFIN ISLAND

USA

CANADA

Lake Superior
Lake Huron

USA

Mississippi–Missouri

Lake Michigan

Vatican City, the world's smallest country, is completely surrounded by Italy's capital city, Rome.

Mexico City ■

Mexico City lies 2,200 m (7,350 ft) above sea level, where the air is exceptionally thin.

Amazon

BRAZIL

N

Kilometres
0 1000 2000 3000 4000

0 1000 2000 3000
Miles

■ **Buenos Aires**

Highest mountains

Mount Everest	Nepal/China	8,848 m/29,028 ft
K2	India	8,611 m/28,250 ft
Kanchenjunga	Nepal/India	8,598 m/28,208 ft
Lhotse I	Nepal/China	8,511 m/27,923 ft
Makalu	Nepal/China	8,481 m/27,824 ft

Longest rivers

Nile	Africa	6,670 km/4,125 mi
Amazon	South America	6,570 km/4,080 mi
Mississippi–Missouri	North America	6,020 km/3,740 mi
Chang Jiang	China	5,900 km/3,722 mi
Yenisei	Russia	5,870 km/3,650 mi

Largest inland waters

Caspian Sea	Central Asia	370,992 sq km/143,241 sq mi
Lake Superior	North America	84,243 sq km/32,526 sq mi
Lake Victoria	Africa	69,500 sq km/26,834 sq mi
Lake Huron	North America	60,700 sq km/23,430 sq mi
Lake Michigan	North America	58,020 sq km/22,395 sq mi

Smallest country by population

Vatican City	Europe	840
Tuvalu	Pacific Ocean	10,300
Nauru	Pacific Ocean	10,390
Palau	Pacific Ocean	15,000
San Marino	Europe	24,000

Largest country by population

China	Asia	1,243,738,000
India	Asia	960,178,000
USA	North America	272,000,000
Indonesia	Asia	203,479,000
Brazil	South America	163,132,000

Russia's land area is 11.5 percent of the land area of the world.

The surface of the **Caspian Sea** is 28 m (92 ft) below sea level.

China's present population is more than that of the whole world 150 years ago!

Mount Everest's height of 8,848 m (29,028 ft) was first measured in 1852 by a British survey team.

The river **Nile** drains about one-tenth of Africa. Lake Victoria is one of its major sources.

Smallest country by area

Vatican City	Europe	0.44 sq km/0.17 sq mi
Monaco	Europe	1.95 sq km/0.75 sq mi
Nauru	Pacific Ocean	21 sq km/8 sq mi
Tuvalu	Pacific Ocean	24 sq km/9.27 sq mi
San Marino	Europe	61 sq km/23.6 sq mi

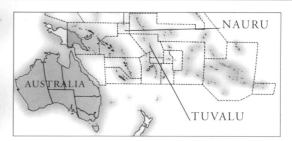

Largest islands

Greenland	Arctic Ocean	2,175,600 sq km/840,325 sq mi
New Guinea	Pacific Ocean	808,510 sq km/312,085 sq mi
Borneo	Pacific Ocean	757,050 sq km/292,220 sq mi
Madagascar	Indian Ocean	587,041 sq km/226,658 sq mi
Baffin Island	Arctic Ocean	476,070 sq km/183,760 sq mi

Largest country by area

Russia	Asia	17,075,400 sq km/6,592,800 sq mi
Canada	North America	9,976,140 sq km/3,851,817 sq mi
China	Asia	9,526,900 sq km/3,676,300 sq mi
USA	North America	9,166,600 sq km/3,539,243 sq mi
Brazil	South America	8,456,508 sq km/3,265,076 sq mi

CANADA
Area: 9,976,140 sq km
Population: 29,942,000

Canada
People and places

Canada is a vast country of forests, mountains, plains and lakes. It is the second biggest country in the world: only Russia has a greater land area. The population of nearly 30 million people is very small for such a big country. Canada's original inhabitants (called First Nations by Canadians), included the Inuit and the aboriginal Native Indian peoples. The Inuit live in small settlements in the cold north of the country, where there are few roads. But most Canadians live in the warmer south, in a narrow band just north of the border with the United States. Here there are big cities such as Toronto, Montreal and Vancouver. New immigrants from many other countries have added to Canada's culture, which for hundreds of years has linked British and French traditions.

THE INUIT

The ancestors of the Inuit crossed from Siberia thousands of years ago. Today, many Inuit have given up their traditional hunting and fishing life to settle in small northern communities.

♦ *The ancestral home of the Inuit is called Nunavut, meaning "Our Land".*

ARCTIC OCEAN

Queen Elizabeth Islands

Banks Island

BEAUFORT SEA

Victoria Island

Arctic Circle

USA (ALASKA)

• Inuvik
Ft. McPherson

Mackenzie

BERING SEA

Great Bear Lake

YUKON TERRITORY

Ft. Norman

MACKENZIE MOUNTAINS

Mt. Logan

NORTHWEST TERRITORIES

⊛ Whitehorse

Yellowknife ⊛

Great Slave Lake

PACIFIC OCEAN

ROCKY MOUNTAINS

Peace

QUEEN CHARLOTTE ISLANDS

• Prince Rupert

ALBERTA

Athabasca

BRITISH COLUMBIA

⊛ Edmonton

N. Saskatchewan

SASKATCHEWAN

⊛ Saskatoon

• Calgary

• Vancouver

Victoria ⊛

S. Saskatchewan

⊛ Regina

Victoria, the capital of British Columbia, is on Vancouver Island. The city of Vancouver is on the mainland.

Canada's border with the United States is the world's longest undefended international boundary.

CANADIAN NATIONAL TOWER

The CN Tower in Toronto is the world's tallest free-standing structure. Built in 1976, it is 553 m (1,814 ft) high. Glass-faced lifts take visitors up to two observation decks, one of which has a see-through floor. You can see Niagara Falls from the top of the Tower.

♦ *Toronto was founded in 1793. Toronto means "meeting place" in the Huron language.*

FRENCH CANADA

There were many French fur traders and farmers among the earliest Europeans to settle in Canada. The French and British fought for control of the country, and the British won in 1760. When the Confederation of Canada was formed in 1867, it allowed French Canadians to govern themselves in the province of Quebec. The famous hotel building called Château Frontenac (right) is in Quebec City, the capital of the province. Most of the people of Quebec speak French, and today many French Canadians want greater independence.

♦ *Canada has two official languages, English and French.*

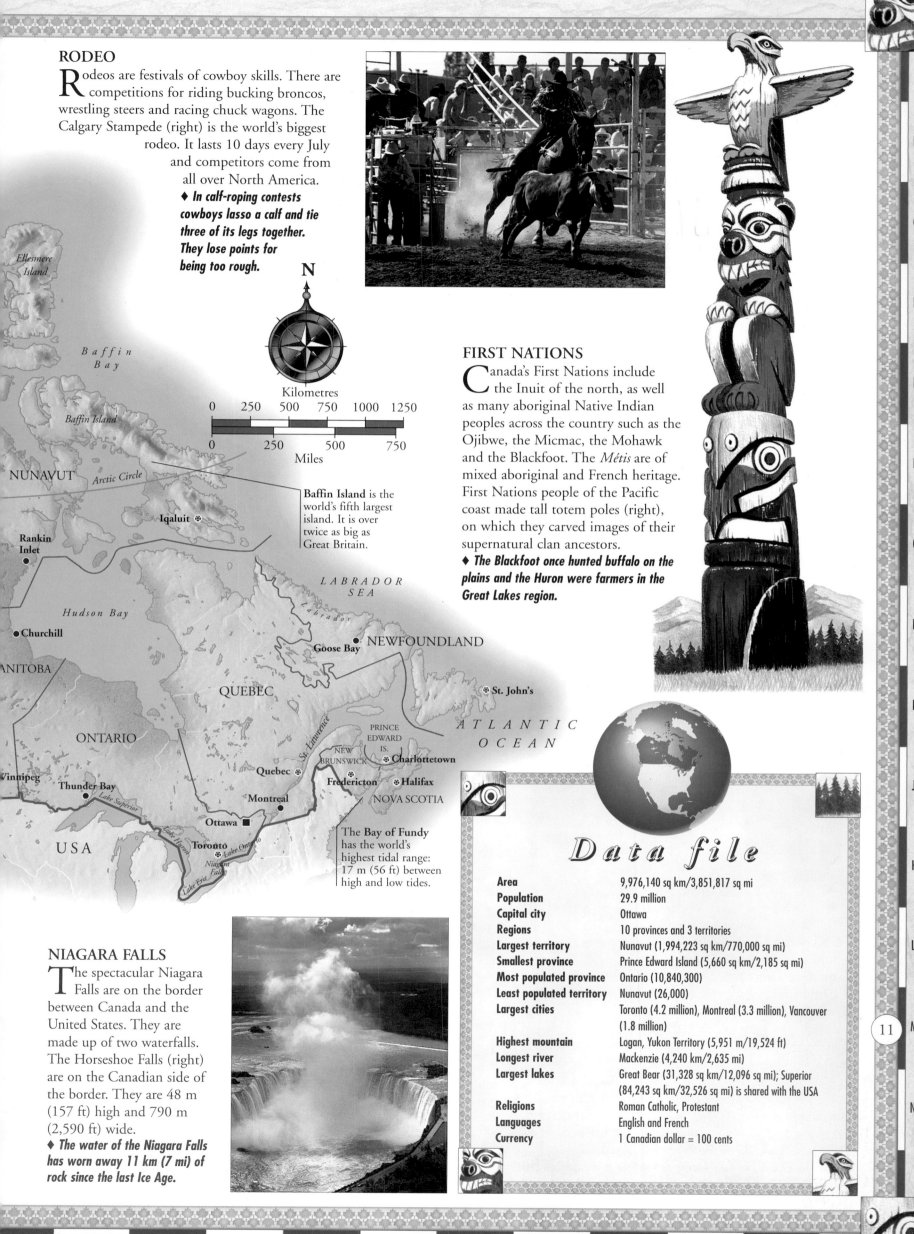

RODEO

Rodeos are festivals of cowboy skills. There are competitions for riding bucking broncos, wrestling steers and racing chuck wagons. The Calgary Stampede (right) is the world's biggest rodeo. It lasts 10 days every July and competitors come from all over North America.

♦ *In calf-roping contests cowboys lasso a calf and tie three of its legs together. They lose points for being too rough.*

N

Kilometres

| 0 | 250 | 500 | 750 | 1000 | 1250 |

| 0 | 250 | 500 | 750 |

Miles

Baffin Island is the world's fifth largest island. It is over twice as big as Great Britain.

Ellesmere Island

Baffin Bay

Baffin Island

NUNAVUT

Arctic Circle

Iqaluit ✧

Rankin Inlet ▪

LABRADOR SEA

Labrador

Hudson Bay

▪**Churchill**

ANITOBA

Goose Bay ▪ NEWFOUNDLAND

QUEBEC

St. John's ✧

ONTARIO

ATLANTIC OCEAN

PRINCE EDWARD IS.

NEW BRUNSWICK

Charlottetown ✧

Quebec ✧

Fredericton ✧ **Halifax** ✧

Vinnipeg

Thunder Bay ▪

Lake Superior

Montreal ▪

NOVA SCOTIA

Ottawa ■

St. Lawrence

The **Bay of Fundy** has the world's highest tidal range: 17 m (56 ft) between high and low tides.

USA

Toronto ✧

Lake Huron *Lake Ontario*

Niagara Falls

Lake Erie

FIRST NATIONS

Canada's First Nations include the Inuit of the north, as well as many aboriginal Native Indian peoples across the country such as the Ojibwe, the Micmac, the Mohawk and the Blackfoot. The *Métis* are of mixed aboriginal and French heritage. First Nations people of the Pacific coast made tall totem poles (right), on which they carved images of their supernatural clan ancestors.

♦ *The Blackfoot once hunted buffalo on the plains and the Huron were farmers in the Great Lakes region.*

NIAGARA FALLS

The spectacular Niagara Falls are on the border between Canada and the United States. They are made up of two waterfalls. The Horseshoe Falls (right) are on the Canadian side of the border. They are 48 m (157 ft) high and 790 m (2,590 ft) wide.

♦ *The water of the Niagara Falls has worn away 11 km (7 mi) of rock since the last Ice Age.*

Data file

Area	9,976,140 sq km/3,851,817 sq mi
Population	29.9 million
Capital city	Ottawa
Regions	10 provinces and 3 territories
Largest territory	Nunavut (1,994,223 sq km/770,000 sq mi)
Smallest province	Prince Edward Island (5,660 sq km/2,185 sq mi)
Most populated province	Ontario (10,840,300)
Least populated territory	Nunavut (26,000)
Largest cities	Toronto (4.2 million), Montreal (3.3 million), Vancouver (1.8 million)
Highest mountain	Logan, Yukon Territory (5,951 m/19,524 ft)
Longest river	Mackenzie (4,240 km/2,635 mi)
Largest lakes	Great Bear (31,328 sq km/12,096 sq mi); Superior (84,243 sq km/32,526 sq mi) is shared with the USA
Religions	Roman Catholic, Protestant
Languages	English and French
Currency	1 Canadian dollar = 100 cents

Canada:
Nature, farming and industry

Canada is rich in natural resources such as timber, minerals and oil. Some of these are found in the remote treeless plains of the tundra in the far north. In order to exploit the natural resources, engineers have built long railways, roads and canals for transportation, and huge dams to make electricity. National parks have been set up to protect the local wildlife from disturbance. Caribou live on the tundra, and in the forests there are bears, moose and beavers. Fishing is an important industry along the coasts, and on the central prairies there are huge wheat fields surrounding isolated farmsteads.

TIMBER TRAIN

Canada's farm and forest products have to be moved long distances to factories and cities, or to ports for shipment abroad. Long goods trains, like this one in the Rocky Mountains of British Columbia (above), are used. Two big Canadian rail companies, CP Rail and CN North America, haul over 100,000 million tonnes (98,420 million tons) of freight a year. In the mountains, many tunnels and bridges had to be built to carry the railway track.

♦ *The original Canadian Pacific Railway opened in 1885. It ran all the way from the Atlantic coast to the Pacific coast.*

FISHING BEARS

Brown bears, often called grizzly bears (right), will eat almost anything, including meat, fruit, honey, insects and fish. They live mostly in forested mountain areas where there are fast-flowing rivers. Some catch salmon by grabbing them out of the water as they swim by, some jump in and flip them onto the bank, and others catch them in their jaws as the salmon leap upstream.

♦ *Salmon are born and die in freshwater rivers, but spend half their life in the ocean.*

Caribou

Snow goose

TUNDRA LANDSCAPE

In the vast, flat tundra region of northern Canada the temperature falls well below freezing in winter and the climate is very dry all year round, which means there are no trees. The ground is frozen, and only the upper layer thaws in the short summers. Lichens grow on rocks and frozen ground. They help make thin soils that support grasses, moss and some shrubs. Many birds and animals avoid the harshest conditions by migrating south in winter to warmer regions. Herds of caribou may travel more than 1,000 km (over 600 mi) to the Canadian forests, while snow geese fly to the southern United States.

♦ *In winter caribou use their hooves and antlers to dig through the snow to find lichen and moss to eat.*

Snowshoe hare

PRAIRIE PROVINCES

The prairies are grassland plains that cover much of the provinces of Alberta, Saskatchewan and Manitoba. Rich soils make for huge wheat fields (right). In drier areas there are also vast cattle ranches. The prairies are covered with snow during winter, but in spring a warm wind called the chinook blows off the Rocky Mountains and melts the snow. In the hot summers there can be droughts and fierce dust storms.
♦ *Canada produces 30 million tonnes (29.5 million tons) of wheat a year.*

CHANGING COLOUR

Some Arctic animals change colour from summer to winter to protect themselves from predators. The brown summer coats of Arctic foxes (below) and Arctic hares change to thicker white coats in winter. This helps them to keep warm in the freezing temperatures and also camouflages them against the snowy landscape.
♦ *In winter Arctic foxes have to travel a long way to find food. They hunt for small animals or fish.*

MAKING PAPER

Almost half of Canada is covered by forest, and the country's timber industry is very important. The soft woods of British Columbia, Quebec and Ontario are made into paper. Logs are taken to pulp mills (left), where the bark is stripped off in revolving drums and the wood is chipped by machines. It is then ground up or boiled with chemicals and mixed with water to make pulp. Finally the pulp is strained, dried and rolled into paper.
♦ *Canadian pulp mills produce a third of the world's newsprint.*

Arctic foxes

Ptarmigan

WOLVES OF THE FORESTS

Grey wolves live in woodland and forests right across Canada, including the Rocky Mountains. They live in family groups, which often join together to form packs of more than 20 animals. They may hunt together, helping to bring down large prey such as deer and caribou. On their own they catch rabbits and mice. Each wolf pack has a strict order, and the leading male signals his rank by carrying his tail higher than the others.
♦ *Wolves howl to let their own pack members know where they are, or to warn other packs to keep their distance.*

Arctic lemming

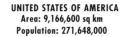

UNITED STATES OF AMERICA
Area: 9,166,600 sq km
Population: 271,648,000

United States of America
People and places

The USA is the fourth largest country in the world and the third most populated. No other country has such an enormous influence on the rest of the world. Hollywood films and American television programmes are watched almost everywhere, and America's industries make many of the things we all buy. But the world has also influenced the United States. People from every continent migrate to the USA, making its cities lively, colourful and varied.

ALASKA
Nicknamed the "Last Frontier", Alaska is a wilderness of high mountains, clear lakes and huge glaciers. It is separated from the rest of the USA by Canada.
♦ *Alaska is the biggest of the 50 states. Texas is the second biggest.*

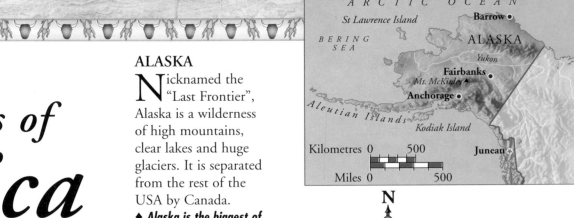

The KTHI television mast in **North Dakota** is the tallest structure in the world. It is 629 m (2,064 ft) high.

HAWAII
This group of islands lies thousands of kilometres from the mainland, in the Pacific Ocean.
♦ *Hawaii became a US state in 1959.*

ON CAPITOL HILL
The Capitol building is in Washington, D.C., capital of the USA. The US Congress meets there to discuss and vote on new laws.
♦ *The US president lives in the White House, near the Capitol.*

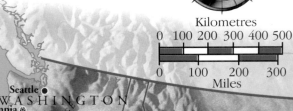

Each American state has its own capital. Phoenix is the capital of Arizona.

TREND-SETTERS
Baseball and skateboarding were invented in America, and rock music was born there. Many popular fast foods are from the USA.
♦ *Los Angeles is the film centre and New York is the centre of fashion.*

Baseball

Skateboard

Hamburger and popcorn

Rock guitar

STATUE OF LIBERTY
This landmark stands on its own island in New York Harbour. It was a gift from the people of France, to celebrate the hundredth anniversary of the US Declaration of Independence in 1776.
♦ *The Statue of Liberty is 45.3 m (148.6 ft) high.*

RAIN DANCE
The Pueblo people of New Mexico (below) dance in the hope that it will rain and help their crops grow. The Pueblos have kept up many traditional ways.
♦ *There are about 2 million Native Americans in the USA.*

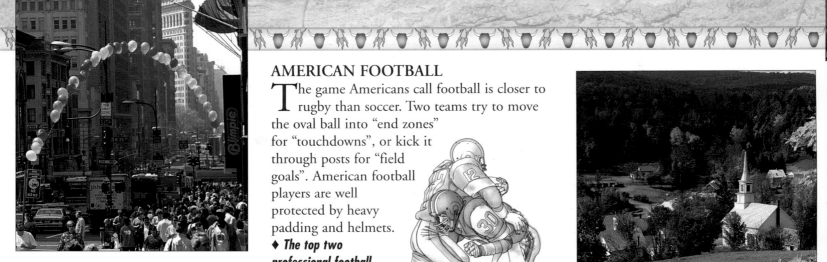

AMERICAN FOOTBALL

The game Americans call football is closer to rugby than soccer. Two teams try to move the oval ball into "end zones" for "touchdowns", or kick it through posts for "field goals". American football players are well protected by heavy padding and helmets.

♦ **The top two professional football teams compete for the annual Super Bowl trophy.**

MIXTURE OF PEOPLE

In New York (above) there are large communities of Puerto Ricans, Italians, Irish, Chinese and others.

♦ **One in twelve Americans was born outside the United States.**

NEW ENGLAND

The gentle hills and beautiful woodlands near the northeast coast of the continent reminded many of the early English settlers of home, so they called the region New England. In states such as Vermont (above) and Massachusetts, they founded small towns and villages. Many of the old traditions of the original settlers have survived to this day.

♦ **The earliest European settlers included Puritans. They arrived on the ship called the Mayflower in 1620 in search of a new life.**

New England is made up of six states: Maine, New Hampshire, Vermont, Massachusetts, Rhode Island and Connecticut.

Data file

Area	9,166,600 sq km/3,539,243 sq mi
Population	272 million
Number of states	50, plus the District of Columbia
Capital city	Washington, D.C. (District of Columbia)
Largest state	Alaska (1,518,748 sq km/586,393 sq mi)
Smallest state	Rhode Island (1,212 sq km/468 sq mi)
Most populated state	California (32,601,000)
Least populated state	Wyoming (484,000)
Largest cities	New York (7.3 million), Los Angeles (3.4 million) Chicago (2.7 million)
Highest mountain	Mount McKinley, Alaska (6,194 m/20,320 ft)
Longest river	Mississippi–Missouri (6,020 km/3,740 mi)
Largest lakes	Michigan (57,757 sq km/22,300 sq mi); Superior (84,243 sq km/32,526 sq mi) is shared with Canada
Religions	Protestant, Roman Catholic, Jewish
Languages	English; also a large Spanish-speaking population
Currency	1 US dollar = 100 cents

How places got their names

Chicago	from a Native American word for *place where wild onions grow*
Florida	from the Spanish, meaning *flowery*
Louisiana	after King Louis XIV of France
Missouri	from the name of a Native American tribe
Virginia	after Elizabeth I of England, the virgin queen

MISSISSIPPI STEAMBOAT

The Mississippi River was important in the development of the USA. People and goods could travel along it, from the heart of the country to New Orleans on the Gulf of Mexico. They were carried on steamboats (below), which were powered by a steam-driven revolving paddle wheel.

♦ **The first steamer, called the New Orleans, ran in 1811. Today, most goods move in barge convoys.**

United States of America:
Nature

The Santa Lucia mountain range rises straight from the Pacific Ocean on the California coast south of San Francisco.

♦ *You can often spot seals and whales from the rocky headlands.*

The American climate varies from the warmth of tropical Florida and Pacific Hawaii to the cold of Arctic Alaska. There are deserts in Arizona and California and forests in the foothills of the Rocky and Appalachian Mountains. The plains across the heart of America are drained by the Mississippi river and its tributaries, including the Missouri. Between the USA and Canada are the five Great Lakes, created when glaciers moved northwards thousands of years ago. Such varying habitats support many different animals. Wolves, bears and mountain lions live in the forests, bison and pronghorns roam across the plains, and there are alligators in the southern swamps.

Pronghorn

Bison

Scarlet mallow

Prairie dog

MONUMENT VALLEY

This breathtaking natural landscape lies high on the Colorado plateau, on the borders of Utah and Arizona. Here the ancient sandstone is harder than the surrounding rocks and so has worn away less. This has left towering pillars and buttes, which glow red and orange in the sun. One rock tower is a volcanic plug, a mass of hard lava left behind when the rest of the volcano wore away.

♦ *The famous film director John Ford shot classic "Westerns" such as Stagecoach and Cheyenne Autumn in Monument Valley.*

SWAMP ALLIGATOR

American alligators live in the Florida Everglades, a large, low-lying area of swamps, mangroves and forests near Miami. In summer, the swamps dry up and alligators go in search of new waterholes.

♦ *Alligators are the direct descendants of reptiles that lived millions of years ago.*

GIANT TREES

Giant sequoias are among the world's biggest and oldest trees. They grow only on the western slopes of the Sierra Nevada mountains in California, in places such as Yosemite National Park (left). The largest sequoia, nicknamed the General Sherman, is 84 m (275 ft) high and 31 m (102 ft) around the base. It may be as much as 2,500 years old.

♦ *A sequoia's thick bark protects it from fire and disease. But lightning can seriously damage the tree.*

NATIONAL PARKS

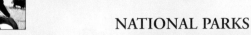

The USA created the world's first national park, Yellowstone, in 1872. There are now 54 American national parks, covering over 2 percent of the country's area. Some of the main ones are shown below. Some parks help to build up numbers of animals, such as bison. Others simply protect animals such as wolves from being hunted. Many parks preserve spectacular natural scenery.

Olympic Park, Washington, preserves a stretch of rugged coastline.

Yellowstone Park, Wyoming, is famous for its hot springs and geysers.

Isle Royale, Michigan, is a large island on Lake Superior where you can see beavers.

Shenandoah, Virginia, is in the beautiful Blue Ridge Mountains.

Yosemite National Park in the Sierra Nevada mountains, California, has jagged peaks and beautiful lakes and waterfalls.

Petrified Forest, Arizona, has ancient trees that have turned into rock.

In Mammoth Cave, Kentucky, you can explore huge caverns.

Bobolink

ON THE GREAT PLAINS

The grasslands of the Great Plains extend right down the USA, from the Canadian border to Texas, and across country from the foothills of the Rockies to the Missouri river. Grasses grow quickly in the short, hot summers, and flowers such as poppies and mallows grow between them. Trees are rare. Vast herds of bison used to roam these plains, but they were hunted almost to extinction. Now those that are left live mainly in parks and reserves. Prairie dogs live together in colonies called "towns", made up of millions of animals.

♦ *The pronghorn can run up to 65 kph (40 mph) across the Great Plains.*

Gopher

MOUNTAIN LION

Mountain lions, sometimes called cougars or pumas, live in the Rocky Mountains. They are lone hunters, each with their own territory ranging up to 50 sq km (19 sq mi). The young are usually born in summer. They stay with their mother for a year or two before venturing off on their own. Mountain lions can leap 6 m (20 ft).

♦ *Mountain lions were once hunted because they were thought to be a danger to cattle. Now they are more protected.*

DAMS AND LODGES

Beavers are good swimmers and can stay under water for up to 15 minutes. They can gnaw through tree trunks with their sharp teeth, and they build dams with the branches. The dams create ponds that make it easier for them to catch fish.

♦ *Beavers build homes, called lodges, out of sticks, mud and stones. The lodges have underwater entrances.*

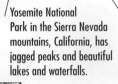

CITY WILDLIFE

When their natural habitats are destroyed by humans, some animals adapt to city life. Raccoons (left) are mischievous animals, hiding out in garages and empty buildings. At night they forage for scraps from dustbins.

♦ *Raccoons are very skilful with their paws and have been known to open refrigerators.*

United States of America:
Farming and industry

Americans manufacture and sell more things than anyone else, which makes the USA the world's biggest economy. They have achieved this powerful position by using their wealth of natural resources wisely, by making many important scientific inventions, and by working hard. There are huge farmlands throughout America, where farmers grow wheat, corn and all kinds of fruit and vegetables, as well as raising cattle, chickens and sheep. In the past, coal and iron ore helped build the country's mighty manufacturing industries. These resources are now running out, but in recent years oil has been found in Alaska and the states around the Gulf of Mexico. New electronics and aircraft industries have also sprung up in Texas, California and Washington. In the big cities there are banks, publishers, film-makers and musicians, all spreading America's influence to the rest of the world.

FIELDS OF CALIFORNIA

Many crops, like these pumpkins, need good soil, plenty of sun and lots of water. California has the soil and sun, but water has to be brought in from wetter areas. Dams, aqueducts and canals transport water from the Sierra Nevada mountains and the Colorado river to the farmlands. Demand is so high that the state is running out of supplies.

♦ *At Halloween, pumpkins are hollowed out and used as lanterns. The pulpy flesh makes pumpkin pie.*

KENNEDY SPACE CENTER

A space shuttle blasts off from Kennedy Space Center (below), at Cape Canaveral in Florida. The shuttle can carry up to seven astronauts and scientists into orbit and back. After two minutes, its two solid fuel rocket boosters drop away and fall to Earth by parachute. Six minutes later its external fuel tank is jettisoned to disintegrate in the atmosphere. When its mission is finished, the shuttle slows down from 28,000 kph (17,400 mph) in space to land back on Earth at 335 kph (208 mph).

♦ *The first man on the Moon was American astronaut Neil Armstrong, in 1969.*

DISNEY

Walt Disney made his first Mickey Mouse cartoon in 1928. Now his company is one of the biggest in the world's entertainment industry, making films such as *The Lion King* and *Hercules*. The company has theme parks in California and Florida (right), as well as in Tokyo and Paris.

♦ *Disney's first long cartoon was Snow White and the Seven Dwarfs, released in 1937.*

LAKESIDE CITY

Chicago, Illinois (right), is the third largest city in the USA. It lies at the southern end of Lake Michigan. The city was founded in 1803 and has changed with the times. It started as a centre for processing and distributing agricultural goods such as grain, timber and meat. Later, it had steel mills and chemical plants. Now it is a financial, printing and educational centre.

♦ *The world's first skyscrapers were built in Chicago, in the 1880s. Now its tallest building is the Sears Tower, which soars to 443 m (1,453 ft).*

CATTLE DRIVE

In the 1800s cowboys herded millions of longhorns along the Chisholm Trail from San Antonio, Texas, to Abilene, Kansas. Today America's main cattle-ranching region is in the drier parts of the Great Plains, from Texas to North Dakota. The cattle are rounded up in autumn (left), taken to feeders for fattening, and then shipped to stockyards for slaughter.

♦ *Americans eat twice as much meat as Europeans.*

TRUCKING

Three-quarters of America's industrial goods are moved by trucks. These trucks, called rigs or semis, have a tractor unit with a driver's cab, and a separate semi-trailer for the cargo. Truck-drivers can travel as much as 150,000 km (93,000 mi) a year. Their cabs often have a bed, a microwave oven and a TV inside.

♦ *US Interstate Highways are numbered. Odd numbers run north–south, such as I-5 from Seattle to San Diego. Even numbers run east–west, such as I-10 from Jacksonville to Los Angeles.*

THE AUTOMOBILE

The mass production of motor cars started in 1913, in Detroit, Michigan. Henry Ford's workers made the first car that most people could afford, called the Model T. The car was nicknamed "Tin Lizzie", and by the early 1920s half the cars in the world were Model T Fords! Detroit is still the centre of the US auto industry, making a quarter of all the cars driven by Americans. Today, the manufacturing process (right) is more automated.

♦ *Americans own 194 million motor vehicles, over a third of the world's total. The three top US car-makers, Ford, General Motors and Chrysler, are among the biggest companies in the world.*

ANTIGUA AND BARBUDA Area: 442 sq km Population: 66,175

BAHAMAS Area: 13,939 sq km Population: 289,000

BARBADOS Area: 430 sq km Population: 262,000

BELIZE Area: 22,965 sq km Population: 224,000

COSTA RICA Area: 51,100 sq km Population: 3,575,000

CUBA Area: 110,861 sq km Population: 11,068,000

DOMINICA Area: 750 sq km Population: 71,000

DOMINICAN REPUBLIC Area: 48,443 sq km Population: 8,097,000

EL SALVADOR Area: 21,041 sq km Population: 5,927,000

Mexico, Central America and the Caribbean
People and places

Mexico is a long, narrow country with the Pacific Ocean to the west and the Gulf of Mexico to the east. To the south are seven smaller countries that form a strip of land known as Central America. Across the Caribbean Sea are the Caribbean islands, or West Indies. Central America was once home to the great civilizations of the Aztecs and the Mayans. After the 1500s, people from all over the world came to the region. On the mainland, the language and religion of the Spanish settlers blended with Native American cultures. British, French and other Europeans settled the islands, bringing slaves from Africa.

OLMEC SCULPTURE

The Olmec civilization was one of the earliest in Central America, lasting from about 1200 to 400 BC. The Olmecs carved giant stone heads, some 3 m (10 ft) high. These may have shown the faces of people sacrificed to Olmec gods.
♦ *The Olmecs worshipped the snake and the jaguar, as the Aztecs did after them.*

For almost 2,000 km (1,240 mi), the border between Mexico and the USA runs along the Rio Grande river. Mexicans call the river the **Rio Bravo**.

Modern **Mexico City** was built on top of the ruins of the Aztec capital of Tenochtitlán.

Map labels: Tijuana, Mexicali, USA, Ciudad Juárez, Hermosillo, Chihuahua, Baja California, Gulf of California, SIERRA MADRE OCCIDENTAL, Rio Bravo/Grande, SIERRA MADRE ORIENTAL, MEXICO, Culiacán, Durango, Monterrey, Matamoros, GULF OF MEXICO, Tropic of Cancer, Aguascalientes, Tampico, León, Guadalajara, Manzanillo, Bay of Campeche, Campeche, Méri, Yucatan Peninsula, Mexico City, Puebla, Veracruz, Citlaltépetl, Belize, Coatzacoalcos, Belmopan, Acapulco, Balsas, Oaxaca, Gulf of Tehuantepec, GUATEMALA, Guatemala City, San Salvador, EL SALVADOR, PACIFIC OCEAN

PIÑATA PARTY

A favourite children's party game in Mexico is smashing the piñata. The piñata is a clay pot or papier-mâché animal suspended by a rope and filled with sweets, fruit and toys. Children, wearing a blindfold, take turns to try and break the piñata with a stick. The treats fall to the ground for all the children to share.
♦ *Every Mexican town and village has its own special fiesta, or holiday, to honour its patron saint.*

MAYAN CITY

Tikal, in Guatemala, was once a great Mayan city with 45,000 inhabitants. Between 200 BC and AD 900 Mayans built stone palaces and stepped pyramids topped by temples (below). They recorded time with complex calendars and made accurate measurements of the sun and moon. The Mayans could also predict eclipses.
♦ *The Tzeltal, Chol and Tojolabal peoples of today are descendants of the Mayans.*

MEXICAN WEAVING

The Mexican state of Oaxaca is home to Zapotecs, Mixtecs and other Native Americans with their own traditional crafts. Zapotec women are famous for weaving shawls and blankets in colourful, detailed designs (left).
♦ *Some villages have specialized in the same designs for centuries.*

20

GRENADA	GUATEMALA	HAITI	HONDURAS	JAMAICA	MEXICO	NICARAGUA	PANAMA	ST KITTS AND NEVIS
Area: 345 sq km Population: 89,000	Area: 108,889 sq km Population: 11,241,000	Area: 27,400 sq km Population: 7,395,000	Area: 112,088 sq km Population: 5,981,000	Area: 10,991 sq km Population: 2,515,000	Area: 1,958,201 sq km Population: 94,280,000	Area: 120,349 sq km Population: 4,351,000	Area: 77,082 sq km Population: 2,722,000	Area: 269 sq km Population: 45,000

CARIBBEAN VILLAGE

This village on the island of St Lucia (left) is typical of the Caribbean. The forest has been cleared for small farms, where people grow vegetables such as cassava, yams and sweet potatoes, and fruits such as plantains and bananas. They sell their produce at markets.

♦ **Many of St Lucia's people are descended from African slaves.**

When Christopher Columbus sailed to the **Caribbean islands** in 1492, he thought he was in the East Indies and called the locals "Indians".

DAY OF THE DEAD

In Mexico, All Souls Day (November 2nd) is celebrated as the Day of the Dead. People visit the graves of their relatives, lighting candles and bringing food offerings. Shops sell sweets and chocolates shaped like skulls (above).

♦ **On December 12th, Mexicans honour Our Lady of Guadalupe, the country's patron saint.**

(Map of the Caribbean region)

BAHAMAS
Nassau
Andros I.
Tropic of Cancer
ATLANTIC OCEAN
Havana
CUBA
Camagüey
Isla de la Juventud
Great Inagua
TURKS & CAICOS ISLANDS (UK)
DOMINICAN REPUBLIC
San Juan
PUERTO RICO (USA)
VIRGIN Is. (US & UK)
ANGUILLA (UK)
ANTIGUA & BARBUDA
ST KITTS & NEVIS
MONTSERRAT (UK)
GUADELOUPE (FR)
DOMINICA
MARTINIQUE (FR)
ST LUCIA
BARBADOS
ST VINCENT & THE GRENADINES
GRENADA
TRINIDAD & TOBAGO
Yucatan Channel
HAITI
Port-au-Prince
Santo Domingo
CAYMAN ISLANDS (UK)
Kingston
JAMAICA
GREATER ANTILLES
LESSER ANTILLES
CARIBBEAN SEA
ARUBA (NETH)
NETHERLANDS ANTILLES (NETH)
BELIZE
HONDURAS
Tegucigalpa
NICARAGUA
Managua
Lake Nicaragua
San José
COSTA RICA
Panama City
Panama Canal
PANAMA
COLOMBIA

N

Kilometres
0 200 400 600 800 1000
0 200 400 600
Miles

PANAMA CANAL

The Panama Canal opened in 1914, allowing ships to pass directly between the Atlantic and Pacific Oceans. This saved them the long journey around South America. The Canal is 81 km (50 mi) long, but is too narrow for many modern ships. A wider canal may be built.

♦ **Over 20,000 workers died from tropical diseases digging the Panama Canal.**

Data file

Area	2,705,661 sq km/1,044,664 sq mi
Population	165 million
Independent countries	21, and 11 dependencies
Largest country	Mexico (1,958,201 sq km/756,067 sq mi)
Smallest country	St Kitts and Nevis (269 sq km/104 sq mi)
Most populated country	Mexico (94,280,000)
Least populated country	St Kitts and Nevis (45,000)
Largest cities	Mexico City, Mexico (15.1 million); Santo Domingo, Dominican Republic (2.5 million)
Highest mountain	Citlaltépetl, Mexico (5,699 m/18,700 ft)
Longest river	Rio Bravo/Grande (3,035 km/1,886 mi), shared with USA
Largest lake	Nicaragua, Nicaragua (8,029 sq km/3,100 sq mi)
Religions	Roman Catholic, Protestant, Hindu
Languages	Spanish, English, French, many Native American languages

How places got their names

Caribbean Sea	after the Carib people
Honduras	from the Spanish *hondas*, meaning depths
Jamaica	from the Arawak for *island of springs*
Martinique	sighted by Columbus on St Martin's Day, June 15th, 1502
Mexico	from the Aztec name for a lake, meaning *lake of the moon*

21

ST LUCIA
Area: 617 sq km
Population: 134,000

ST VINCENT AND THE GRENADINES
Area: 389 sq km
Population: 106,000

TRINIDAD AND TOBAGO
Area: 5,128 sq km
Population: 1,308,000

Mexico, Central America and the Caribbean:
Nature, farming and industry

This is a region of great contrasts, from the dry deserts of northern Mexico to the wet tropical rainforests of Panama. Many kinds of cactus grow in the desert, and there are hummingbirds and orchids in the forest. The volcanic, mountainous islands of the Caribbean are surrounded by warm seas, where turtles and sailfish swim. The islands' rich soils are good for crops such as sugar, coffee and bananas. Tourists come here for the hot sun, sandy beaches and clear blue waters. The Mexican economy, which is the region's richest, has developed thanks to farming, manufacturing and newly discovered oilfields.

VOLCANIC ISLANDS

The larger Caribbean islands are the peaks of an ocean mountain chain. The smaller islands of the Lesser Antilles are volcanic. Although many of these volcanoes are extinct, like the Pitons in St Lucia (above right), some are still active. In 1997 the eruption of Mount Soufriere on Montserrat forced many people to leave the island.
♦ *The western coast of Central America has many volcanoes and earthquakes. Mexico City was devastated by an earthquake in 1985.*

SAILFISH

Sailfish live in the tropical waters of the Caribbean Sea. They are powerful swimmers and are the fastest of all fish. They can reach a speed of 100 kph (62 mph).
♦ *The fin on a fish's back is called the dorsal fin. Sailfish have an especially big dorsal fin, and a long, swordlike beak.*

IN THE DESERT

The Sonoran Desert stretches across northern Mexico and into the USA. Despite the high temperatures and low rainfall, many plants and animals manage to survive in these extreme conditions. The saguaro cactus, for example, stores water in its thick trunk; jackrabbits have big ears that help to let heat escape from their bodies; and snakes and mice hide in burrows by day and only come out to feed at night.
♦ *Although the roadrunner can fly, it prefers to scurry very fast over the ground.*

Eagle

Saguaro cactus

Roadrunner

Jackrabbit

Gila monster

HURRICANE!

Hurricanes are very fierce tropical storms. They often start out in the Atlantic, before moving across the Caribbean Sea and the Gulf of Mexico. Winds can reach 120 kph (75 mph), causing great damage on land to crops and buildings, as well as loss of life.
♦ *The centre of a hurricane, where wind speeds are lowest, is called the "eye".*

Path of hurricane

TRADITIONAL FOODS

Mexican farmers grow about 50 different kinds of beans, which are used in many traditional dishes. Maize, which we also call corn, and squash are also common throughout Central America and the Caribbean.

♦ *A squash is a large vegetable similar to a pumpkin.*

Beans   Maize   Squash

MEXICAN OIL

Mexico is one of the world's leading oil producers. Oil is found along the Gulf coast and is also extracted from offshore drilling rigs. The crude oil is processed at refineries like this one at Tula (left). Oil is a major source of income for Mexico.

♦ *Trinidad and Tobago also has oil reserves, and its refineries process oil from Venezuela.*

FOREST LIFE

Forests cover much of southern Central America. Some are hot and steamy all year round. Others, such as the cloud forests of Costa Rica, which grow at 900 to 1,500 m (2,950 to 4,900 ft) above sea level, are damp and cold, and the trees are covered in lichens and moss. Along the western coast of Mexico, where the forests are sheltered from the strong northeasterly winds, they are much drier. Millions of years ago, North and South America were separated by ocean. When falling sea levels created a land bridge, animals and plants crossed and mixed together in Central America. Today, there may be hundreds of different bird species and thousands of different insect species in a small area of forest.

♦ *Bats thrive in Central America's forests. Panama alone has 31 different species. Some eat fruit, others drink nectar, and a few, like the vampire bat, are carnivores.*

Howler monkey

Squirrel monkey

Quetzal

Fruit bat

Ocelot

Hummingbird

Poison-arrow frog

MAKING SISAL

The agave plant is common in the Yucatan peninsula of Mexico. Its leaves are cut, and the fibres inside are taken out and dried (above) to make sisal.

♦ *Sisal is used to make ropes.*

CARIBBEAN TOURISM

Because of their ideal climate and warm waters, the Caribbean islands are a favourite holiday destination. Tourists enjoy places like this beach resort on St Thomas (above), one of the US Virgin Islands.

♦ *The smaller Virgin Islands are uninhabited.*

ARGENTINA	BOLIVIA	BRAZIL	CHILE	COLOMBIA	ECUADOR	GUYANA	PARAGUAY	PERU
Area: 2,780,092 sq km Population: 35,671,000	Area: 1,098,581 sq km Population: 7,774,000	Area: 8,456,508 sq km Population: 163,132,000	Area: 756,626 sq km Population: 14,624,000	Area: 1,141,748 sq km Population: 37,067,000	Area: 269,178 sq km Population: 11,938,000	Area: 215,083 sq km Population: 847,000	Area: 406,752 sq km Population: 5,088,000	Area: 1,285,216 sq km Population: 24,367,000

South America
People and places

METALWORKING

Metalwork dating from 1500 BC has been found in the Andes. This pendant was made about AD 1000.

♦ **Gold was panned from mountain rivers.**

Modern South America is built on the ruins of ancient civilizations, and is a mixture of traditional Native American villages and huge, rapidly growing cities. Brazil and Argentina have some of the biggest cities in the world. The people of South America are a mixture of the descendants of Spanish and Portuguese colonists and native peoples such as the Quechua, who are descendants of the Incas. Half the population of South America lives in Brazil, which covers nearly half the continent.

The delta of the river **Amazon** is over 300 km (186 mi) across and extends 400 km (250 mi) inland.

Lake Titicaca is the highest navigable lake in the world (3,811 m/ 12,503 ft).

BUENOS AIRES

The capital of Argentina (left) is also the country's main port and industrial centre. With large communities of Italians, Spaniards, Germans and Britons, some districts resemble a European city.

♦ **Natives of Buenos Aires are porteños, "people of the port".**

PEOPLE OF THE ANDES

Many of the Native Americans who live in the Andes mountains are farmers. They grow grain and potatoes, and herd animals such as sheep and llamas (below, in a village in Bolivia). Life can be very tough in these steep mountains, where many villages have no electricity.

♦ **The Quechua and the Aymará people make up half of Bolivia's population.**

Cape Horn, where the Pacific Ocean meets the Atlantic, is known to sailors for its violent storms.

The **Falkland Islands** are a self-governing British colony, called Islas Malvinas by the Argentinians.

Kilometres
0 200 400 600 800 1000

0 200 400 600
Miles

FALKLAND ISLANDS (UK)

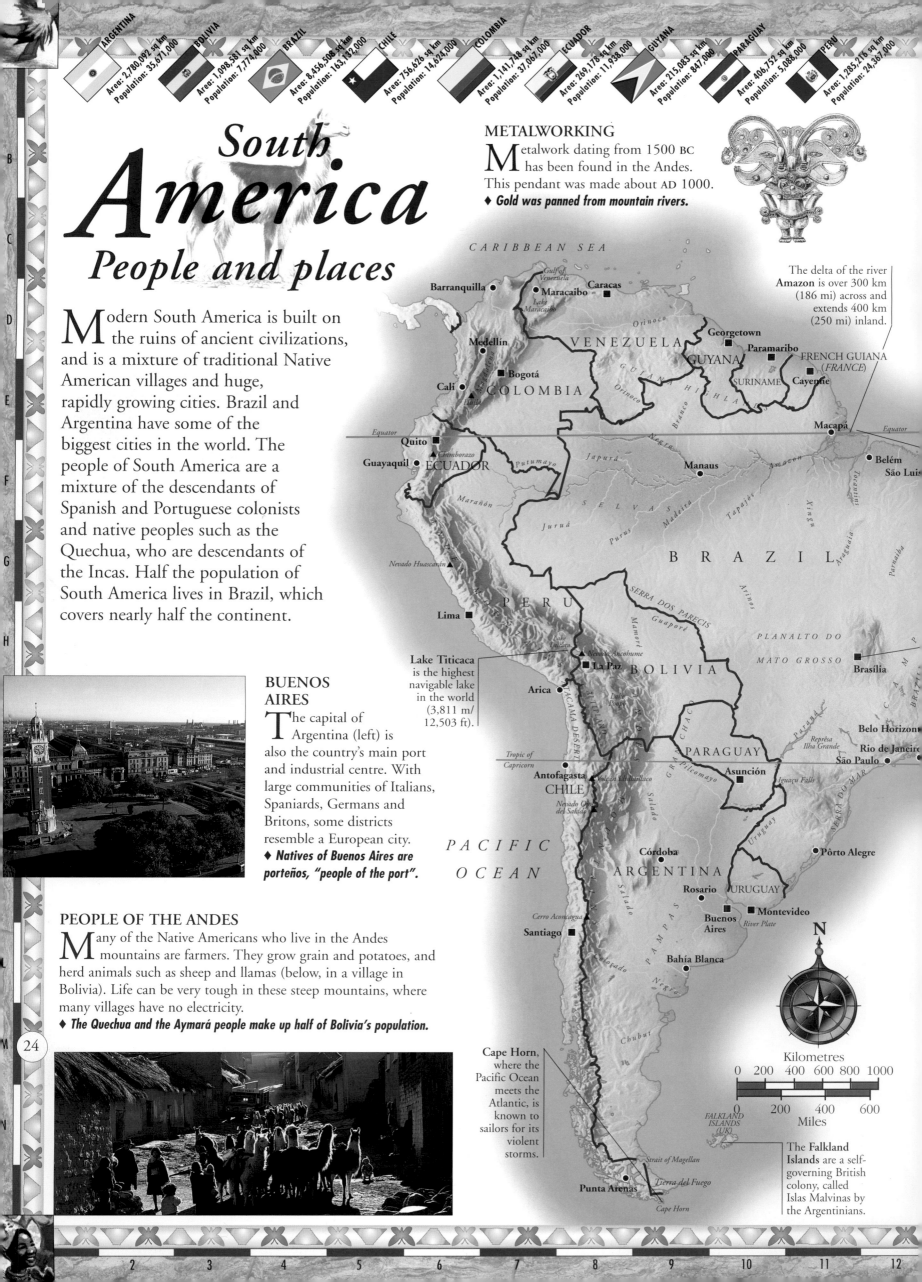

Map labels: CARIBBEAN SEA, Barranquilla, Maracaibo, Caracas, Gulf of Venezuela, Lake Maracaibo, Orinoco, VENEZUELA, Georgetown, Paramaribo, FRENCH GUIANA (FRANCE), GUYANA, SURINAME, Cayenne, Medellín, GUIANA HIGHLANDS, Bogotá, Cali, COLOMBIA, Orinoco, Equator, Quito, Chimborazo, ECUADOR, Guayaquil, Putumayo, Japurá, Negro, Macapá, Equator, Belém, São Luis, Marañón, Manaus, Amazon, SELVAS, Juruá, Madeira, Tapajós, Xingu, Tocantins, Nevado Huascarán, Purus, BRAZIL, PERU, Juruá, Serra dos Parecis, Guaporé, Arinos, Araguaia, Parnaíba, Lima, Lake Titicaca, Nevado Ancohuma, PLANALTO DO MATO GROSSO, La Paz, BOLIVIA, Brasília, Arica, Lake Poopó, ATACAMA DESERT, ALTIPLANO, GRAN CHACO, Belo Horizonte, Represa Ilha Grande, Tropic of Capricorn, PARAGUAY, Rio de Janeiro, Antofagasta, Volcán Llullaillaco, CHILE, Pilcomayo, Asunción, Iguaçu Falls, SERRA DO MAR, São Paulo, Nevado Ojos del Salado, Salado, Paraná, Uruguay, Pôrto Alegre, PACIFIC OCEAN, Córdoba, ARGENTINA, URUGUAY, Cerro Aconcagua, Rosario, Montevideo, PAMPAS, River Plate, Santiago, Buenos Aires, Salado, Bahía Blanca, Colorado, Negro, Chubut, N, Strait of Magellan, Tierra del Fuego, Punta Arenas, Cape Horn

SURINAME
Area: 163,820 sq km
Population: 437,000

URUGUAY
Area: 175,016 sq km
Population: 3,222,000

VENEZUELA
Area: 912,050 sq km
Population: 22,777,000

INCA RUINS

All that is left of Machu Picchu (left) in Peru is ruins, but once it was a holy city of the mighty Inca empire. The Incas ruled over the people of the Andes from Colombia to northern Chile. They built suspension bridges, which were unknown in Europe, and cut stone blocks with such precision that their buildings and palaces needed no mortar. Their empire was destroyed by Spanish invaders in 1532.

♦ *Machu Picchu was mysteriously abandoned by the Incas and rediscovered in 1911.*

FOREST PEOPLE

The Yanomami are the largest forest tribe, and they are among the last to give up their traditional ways. They live in villages in the Amazon rainforest (below), on the border of Brazil and Venezuela. Like many other forest peoples, their numbers were once much greater. Only about 19,000 are left. Many died from diseases such as smallpox, brought by Europeans, and miners invaded their lands in search of gold.

♦ *In 1998 fires swept through many parts of the Amazon rainforest destroying Yanomami lands.*

ATLANTIC OCEAN

• Fortaleza

• Recife

São Francisco

ragem de
radinho

Maceió •

alvador •

Tropic of
Capricorn

Where the river **Amazon** enters the sea, fresh water flows 250 km (155 mi) out into the Atlantic.

In 1960, **Brasília** replaced Rio de Janeiro as the capital of Brazil.

RIO CARNIVAL

The annual carnival in Rio de Janeiro, Brazil, is a festival of colourful parades, fancy-dress parties and samba. This exciting form of music and dance was invented in Brazil, blending African and European rhythms.

♦ *Carnival is based on a Christian tradition of feasting before the period of fasting called Lent.*

FOOTBALL CRAZY

One thing that unites South America is a passion for soccer. The continent has some of the biggest stadiums and most fanatical soccer fans in the world. South American teams and players such as Pelé, Maradona and Ronaldo rank among the best to have played the game. Soccer was introduced by British railway engineers in the early 1900s. Uruguay was the first country to host football's top competition, the World Cup, in 1930.

♦ *Since 1930, Brazil has proved to be the most successful World Cup soccer nation.*

Data file

Area	17,763,843 sq km/6,858,673 sq mi
Population	327 million
Independent countries	12, and 2 dependencies
Largest country	Brazil (8,456,508 sq km/3,265,076 sq mi)
Smallest country	Suriname (163,820 sq km/63,251 sq mi)
Most populated country	Brazil (163,132,000)
Least populated country	Suriname (437,000)
Largest cities	Buenos Aires, Argentina (11.6 million); São Paulo, Brazil (9.6 million); Rio de Janeiro, Brazil (5.5 million)
Highest mountain	Aconcagua, Argentina (6,960 m/22,834 ft)
Longest river	Amazon (6,570 km/4,080 mi)
Largest lake	Maracaibo, Venezuela (13,261 sq km/5,120 sq mi)
Religions	Roman Catholic, Protestant
Languages	Spanish, Portuguese, Native American languages

How places got their names

Amazon	from a Native American word for *big wave*
Bogotá	after a Native American chief
Brazil	from the Portuguese for *red wood dye*
Buenos Aires	from the Spanish for *good winds*, short for Nuestra Señora Santa Maria del Buen Aire, the patron saint of sailors
Tierra del Fuego	from the Spanish for *land of fires*, after the Portuguese explorer Ferdinand Magellan saw bonfires on the shore
Venezuela	from Spanish, meaning *little Venice*

25

South America: *Nature*

S outh America has two great natural features that shape the landscape: the Andes mountains and the river Amazon. The Andes extend all the way down the western edge of the continent, from warm, tropical Colombia to the cold lands of southern Chile and Argentina. The Amazon begins high in the Peruvian Andes, not far from the Pacific Ocean, and flows through a huge tropical rainforest all the way to the Atlantic. It is the world's second longest river and drains an area half the size of the United States. South America also has grasslands, swamps and cold deserts. These amazing landscapes are home to a greater variety of wildlife than any other continent.

IN THE ANDES MOUNTAINS

T he mountains of the Andes rise steeply from the Pacific coast. The rapid changes in altitude mean that the slopes have many different habitats. There are farmlands in the foothills, which give way to high, empty plains. Higher up there are glaciers and snow-covered peaks, even close to the Equator. This view over the Chilean Andes (above) was taken from the Orsono volcano.

♦ *The Andes is the world's longest mountain range, at 7,200 km (4,470 mi).*

ATACAMA DESERT

W ind-sculpted rock formations and salt deposits are found in the Valley of the Moon (left), in the Atacama Desert. This part of northern Chile is very rich in minerals. The cool, barren lands of the Atacama are probably the driest place on Earth. In some areas of the desert rain has never been known to fall.

♦ *Plants grow even in the Atacama Desert. Some flowers are able to use moisture from coastal fogs.*

IGUAÇU FALLS

T he spectacular Iguaçu Falls, in southern Brazil, are made up of 275 cascades. Water plunges over the Paraná Plateau, across a gulf 4 km (2.5 mi) wide. Their name means "great waters" in the language of the local Guaraní people.

♦ *Near the Falls is one of the world's biggest dams, Itaipú, built jointly by Brazil and Paraguay.*

THE GALÁPAGOS ISLANDS

T hese unique islands lie about 1,000 km (620 mi) off the coast of Ecuador. When the naturalist, Charles Darwin, visited the islands in 1835, he saw that species of animals there were slightly different from those on the mainland. From his observations Darwin developed a theory of evolution – that tiny changes in a species over long periods of time lead to major variations and even new species. The marine iguana of the Galápagos is the only lizard that swims in the sea.

♦ *The islands take their name from the galápago, or giant tortoise.*

Marine iguana

San Salvador

Fernandina

Santa Cruz

Isabela

San Cristóbal

Santa Maria

Espanola

Frigate bird

Giant tortoise

Galápagos Islands

THE SHRINKING FOREST

The Amazon rainforest covers about 6 million sq km (2.3 million sq mi) across parts of nine countries. But it is being cleared at an alarming rate. Cattle ranches, farms, dams and mines eat into the forest. Deforestation causes many problems. It leads to flooding, soil erosion and the extinction of animals and plants, forcing native peoples to change their way of life. Massive burning of trees adds to the greenhouse gases that cause global warming.

One fifth of the world's bird species are found in the Amazon rainforest.

Dams built at Tucuruí and Balbina flooded large areas of land and drowned the forests.

Brazil is the world's second largest producer of tropical timber, after India.

In 10 sq km (4 sq mi) of rainforest, there may be up to 1,500 different species of flowers, 400 species of birds and 150 species of butterflies.

As many as 90 Amazonian tribes disappeared in the 1900s, as parts of the rainforest were cleared.

Between 1960 and 1990 almost a fifth of South America's tropical rainforest cover was cleared.

- Tropical forest
- Deforested areas

LIFE IN THE TROPICAL RAINFOREST

Tropical forests such as the Amazon rainforest are warm and wet all year round. These conditions mean that rainforests are full of life. A tenth of the world's species of animals and plants may live there. The trees are so dense that little light reaches the forest floor. Toucans and macaws fly through the forest, and monkeys swing through the trees using their tails as a fifth limb. Bird-eating spiders have a leg-span of up to 20 cm (8 in), and they hunt small mammals and birds.

♦ *The jaguar usually hunts at night. This big cat is an excellent swimmer and often catches fish.*

MAGELLAN PENGUINS

Magellan penguins live at the southern tip of South America and off the Falkland Islands. They lay their eggs in burrows or under rocks. Because the summer is so short and the winter so cold, the chicks have to grow up fast.

♦ *Magellan penguins are closely related to the Galápagos species, the most northerly of all penguins.*

Macaw

Sloth

Tamarin

Vampire bat

Bird-eating spider

Toucan

Jaguar

South America:
Farming and industry

South America is often thought of as being part of the developing world, but it does not lack resources and industries. It has modern, thriving cities, though many city-dwellers live in poor housing. Brazil's economy is bigger than that of Russia. It is a major steel producer and makes as many cars as Britain. South American countries grow and export many foods and farm products. Coffee, cocoa, sugar and soya beans are grown on large plantations. Brazil produces more fruit than any other country, including oranges, pineapples and bananas. Small farmers grow cassava in warm areas and potatoes in the mountains. Mountain people also herd llamas and alpacas for their meat and wool. Forest-dwellers tap rubber trees and gather nuts, fruit and honey for sale at markets. South America also has many deposits of minerals and fossil fuels.

GAUCHOS
Gauchos are Argentina's cowboys, famous for their horsemanship. They herd cattle on the country's vast pampas, or grassy plains. They wear black hats and riding trousers called bombachas.
♦ *Argentina and Brazil are both major beef-producing countries.*

GROWING COFFEE
Coffee comes from a shrub, or small tree, that grows best in highland regions in the Tropics (below). The shrubs produce berries that look like bright red cherries. These are picked by hand or by a machine that shakes the berries off the trees, and then the outer pulp is removed. Inside each coffee berry are two beans. These beans are dried in the sun before the last of the skin is removed. The coffee beans are then roasted in big ovens, and some of them are ground to make instant coffee.
♦ *Brazil and Colombia are the world's two leading producers of coffee. The coffee plant originally grew in East Africa.*

TOY MAKING
The Amerindians of South America made toys out of the things they found around them. They made dolls from dried corn husks and sticks. Around Lake Titicaca, children were given tiny models of the reed boats that sailed on the lake. In Colombia, people made ceramic birds, while Brazilians crafted pottery whistles shaped like animals. The tradition is kept alive today, but with more modern toys like buses (right), cars and planes.
♦ *The toys made by people of the Xingu region of Brazil are highly prized by museums and collectors around the world.*

COMMON CROPS
Some foods that are eaten every day around the world came from South America. They were taken to Europe by Spanish conquerors in the 1500s. Today manioc, also called cassava, is an important part of the diet of many Africans. Potatoes are the world's most commonly grown vegetable, and tomatoes are popular everywhere.
♦ *Potatoes are rich in starch, high in protein and contain important vitamins and minerals.*

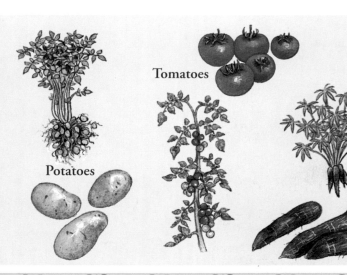

Tomatoes

Potatoes

Manioc

BUILDING AIRCRAFT

Brazil is the main manufacturing country in South America and the world's tenth largest industrial economy. Brazilian industry has grown rapidly since the 1960s. Much of it is based on local raw materials. The government helped industries such as clothing, textiles, food processing and shipbuilding, and started joint ventures with foreign companies to build cars. It also helped set up a company to build small aircraft. There are few good roads in many regions of Brazil, so people rely on planes to get to remote areas. Brazil also makes military planes (below) and has become the world's sixth largest manufacturer of aircraft.

♦ *Brazilian industry is centred on the region around São Paulo, which produces 80 percent of the country's industrial goods.*

FISHING

The Pacific waters off the coast of Peru and Chile contain some of the world's richest fishing grounds. The Humboldt current brings cold water from the south that is rich in plankton, the tiny shrimplike creatures on which many fish feed. Peruvian trawlers catch large quantities of sardines and anchovies, and individual fishermen make much bigger catches (below). Chileans catch hake, swordfish, sole and conger eels.

♦ *Peru's fish catch goes down when its cold waters are occasionally replaced by warmer tropical currents.*

MINING AND MINERALS

The native peoples of South America worked with precious metals, and the Spanish colonists searched for gold, silver and tin. Many of the old mines are now exhausted, but minerals continue to be very important to the continent's economies. Brazil is the largest producer of iron ore in the world. Copper makes up 40 percent of Chile's exports. Venezuela is a leading oil producer, and new oilfields have been discovered in Colombia and Peru.

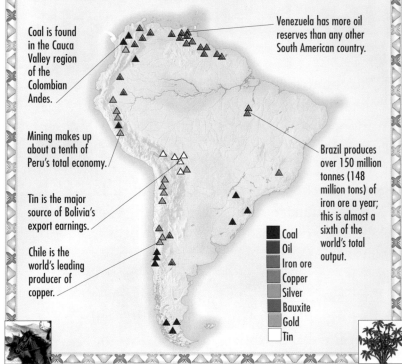

Coal is found in the Cauca Valley region of the Colombian Andes.

Venezuela has more oil reserves than any other South American country.

Mining makes up about a tenth of Peru's total economy.

Tin is the major source of Bolivia's export earnings.

Chile is the world's leading producer of copper.

Brazil produces over 150 million tonnes (148 million tons) of iron ore a year; this is almost a sixth of the world's total output.

- Coal
- Oil
- Iron ore
- Copper
- Silver
- Bauxite
- Gold
- Tin

CHILEAN COPPER

The world's largest open-cast copper mine is in Chuquicamata, Chile (above). The giant hole in the ground measures 4.8 km by 2.5 km (3 mi by 1.6 mi), and half of all Chile's copper comes from this one mine. Dynamite is used to blast out the ore, which is then loaded onto giant trucks. Each day 150 trucks take away 550,000 tonnes (541,000 tons) of ore. They take it to a plant where it is crushed, mixed with water and then mashed. Chemicals are used to separate the copper, as well as other minerals such as silver. The copper is then smelted at high temperatures into ingots. This process creates dangerous by-products, such as sulphur and arsenic.

♦ *Copper can be shaped quite easily and is a good conductor of heat and electricity. This makes it ideal for making wire and electrical components.*

DENMARK Area: 43,093 sq km Population: 5,248,000

ESTONIA Area: 45,100 sq km Population: 1,455,000

FINLAND Area: 338,145 sq km Population: 5,142,000

ICELAND Area: 103,000 sq km Population: 274,000

IRELAND Area: 70,285 sq km Population: 3,559,000

LATVIA Area: 64,500 sq km Population: 2,475,000

LITHUANIA Area: 65,200 sq km Population: 3,719,000

NORWAY Area: 323,878 sq km Population: 4,364,000

SWEDEN Area: 449,964 sq km Population: 8,844,000

Northern *Europe*
People and places

The countries of northern Europe all have distinct identities, but they also have many things in common. The people of Iceland, Norway, Sweden, Denmark and the Faeroe Islands are descendants of the Vikings, and their languages are all derived from Old Norse, the language of the Vikings. English, the main language of the United Kingdom and Ireland, also contains many Norse words, because Vikings settled there in the 8th and 9th centuries. The three Baltic states of Lithuania, Latvia and Estonia were part of the former Soviet Union until 1991, when they regained their independence. They have particularly strong traditions of music and folk art.

TRADITIONAL WAYS

Along the rugged coasts and on the islands of northern Europe, people farm and fish in traditional ways. This Faeroe islander (right) is shearing a sheep.
♦ **The Faeroes are a group of 22 islands. They belong to Denmark.**

Kilometres
0 100 200 300 400 500

0 100 200 300
Miles

Vatnajökullia is a huge icecap on Iceland. It covers eight percent of the country.

STONEHENGE

Stonehenge is a mysterious ancient stone circle in southern England. There are at least three monuments on the site, built by different peoples between about 3000 and 1500 BC. No one really knows what they were for. The stones might have been used as a calendar or as a means of predicting eclipses of the sun and moon.
♦ **Some of the giant stones were brought all the way from the mountains of Wales.**

Scotland voted to have its own parliament in 1997, but it remains a part of the United Kingdom.

Cork is the second largest city in the Republic of Ireland, after Dublin. It was originally a Viking stronghold.

A barrier has been built across the river **Thames** to protect London from flooding.

SENTRY DUTY

The British have many colourful ceremonies associated with the royal family. This sentry is a member of one of the seven army regiments that take turns to guard the Queen. Every June there is a spectacular parade called the "Trooping of the Colour" near Buckingham Palace in London by the Guards, in the presence of the Queen.
♦ **Norway, Sweden and Denmark also have royal families.**

TOWN AND COUNTRY

Britain changed from a farming to an industrial nation during the 1700s. In about 1850 it became the first country in which the majority of people lived in cities rather than villages. But rural life is still very important. Widecombe in the Moor in southwest England (right) is a typical English village. Its church tower dates from the 16th century.
♦ **Many of Britain's favourite paintings, poems and TV series focus on village life.**

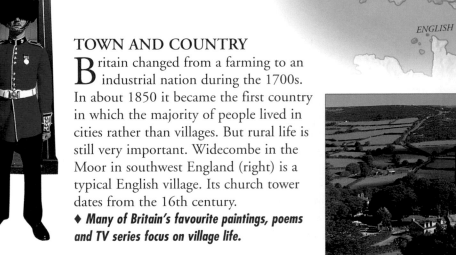

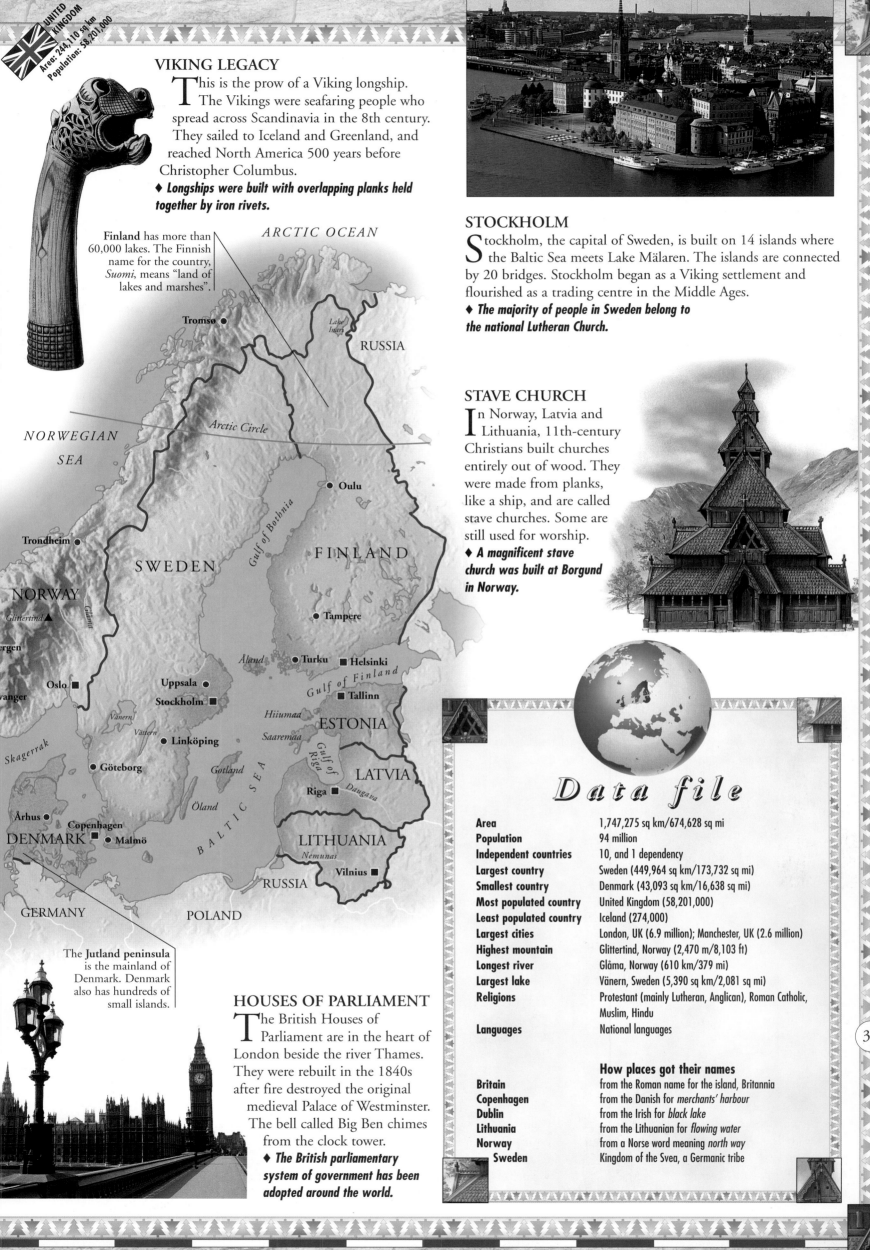

VIKING LEGACY

This is the prow of a Viking longship. The Vikings were seafaring people who spread across Scandinavia in the 8th century. They sailed to Iceland and Greenland, and reached North America 500 years before Christopher Columbus.

♦ *Longships were built with overlapping planks held together by iron rivets.*

Finland has more than 60,000 lakes. The Finnish name for the country, *Suomi*, means "land of lakes and marshes".

STOCKHOLM

Stockholm, the capital of Sweden, is built on 14 islands where the Baltic Sea meets Lake Mälaren. The islands are connected by 20 bridges. Stockholm began as a Viking settlement and flourished as a trading centre in the Middle Ages.

♦ *The majority of people in Sweden belong to the national Lutheran Church.*

STAVE CHURCH

In Norway, Latvia and Lithuania, 11th-century Christians built churches entirely out of wood. They were made from planks, like a ship, and are called stave churches. Some are still used for worship.

♦ *A magnificent stave church was built at Borgund in Norway.*

Map labels
ARCTIC OCEAN
Tromsø
Lake Inari
RUSSIA
NORWEGIAN SEA
Arctic Circle
Oulu
Trondheim
SWEDEN
FINLAND
NORWAY
Glittertind ▲
Tampere
Bergen
Åland
Turku
Helsinki
Stavanger
Oslo
Uppsala
Gulf of Finland
Stockholm
Tallinn
Vänern
Vättern
Hiiumaa
ESTONIA
Skagerrak
Saaremaa
Linköping
Gulf of Riga
Göteborg
Gotland
LATVIA
Öland
Riga
Daugava
Århus
BALTIC SEA
Copenhagen
LITHUANIA
DENMARK
Malmö
Nemunas
Vilnius
RUSSIA
GERMANY
POLAND
Gulf of Bothnia
Glåma

The **Jutland peninsula** is the mainland of Denmark. Denmark also has hundreds of small islands.

HOUSES OF PARLIAMENT

The British Houses of Parliament are in the heart of London beside the river Thames. They were rebuilt in the 1840s after fire destroyed the original medieval Palace of Westminster. The bell called Big Ben chimes from the clock tower.

♦ *The British parliamentary system of government has been adopted around the world.*

Data file

Area	1,747,275 sq km/674,628 sq mi
Population	94 million
Independent countries	10, and 1 dependency
Largest country	Sweden (449,964 sq km/173,732 sq mi)
Smallest country	Denmark (43,093 sq km/16,638 sq mi)
Most populated country	United Kingdom (58,201,000)
Least populated country	Iceland (274,000)
Largest cities	London, UK (6.9 million); Manchester, UK (2.6 million)
Highest mountain	Glittertind, Norway (2,470 m/8,103 ft)
Longest river	Glåma, Norway (610 km/379 mi)
Largest lake	Vänern, Sweden (5,390 sq km/2,081 sq mi)
Religions	Protestant (mainly Lutheran, Anglican), Roman Catholic, Muslim, Hindu
Languages	National languages

How places got their names

Britain	from the Roman name for the island, Britannia
Copenhagen	from the Danish for *merchants' harbour*
Dublin	from the Irish for *black lake*
Lithuania	from the Lithuanian for *flowing water*
Norway	from a Norse word meaning *north way*
Sweden	Kingdom of the Svea, a Germanic tribe

Northern Europe:
Nature, farming and industry

Northern Europe stretches from the Arctic to the mild, rainy lowlands of Britain and Ireland. While Iceland is a cold plateau with active volcanoes, Norway and Sweden are mainly mountainous and forested. Finland and the Baltic countries of Estonia, Latvia and Lithuania are low-lying areas of lakes, rivers and woodlands. The region's uplands are dominated by sheep farming and forestry, while the lowlands contain mechanized farms that produce dairy goods and food crops. Compared with other parts of the world, few people in northern Europe work in farming and fishing. Most live and work in cities. Sweden and the United Kingdom are important manufacturing countries, while Norway has become rich from its oil and natural gas.

BALTIC SEAL

Seals are mammals that live most of their lives in the sea, although they return to land to breed and sleep. Their limbs are flippers, and they have waterproof fur. Layers of blubber under their skin help keep them warm in icy waters. The Baltic seal (right) lives around the coasts of Finland.

♦ *On land seals are slow-moving and vulnerable to animal predators and human hunters. But in the sea they are fast, powerful swimmers.*

NORTH SEA OIL

Oil was discovered under the North Sea in 1970. Soon special production platforms were installed, mainly in the waters of Norway, the United Kingdom and Denmark. Gullfaks C (left) is a huge Norwegian oil and natural gas platform, with a large accommodation block for its workers. Many of the North Sea oilfields are now running low, but new oil has been found in the Atlantic west of the Shetland Islands.

♦ *The crude oil that is extracted is refined into fuel for cars and aeroplanes.*

SCANDINAVIAN FURNITURE

Wood is one of the most valuable resources of Scandinavia. Two-thirds of Finland and half of Sweden are covered in forest. The trees are mostly coniferous softwoods such as pine and spruce, and there is also a lot of birch. These trees grow quickly and are easy to cut and shape, which makes them ideal for making furniture. Sweden is one of the world's leading furniture manufacturers.

♦ *Many of Scandinavia's forests are managed by companies that replant after cutting. The logs are transported by fast-flowing rivers to the sawmills.*

GIANT'S CAUSEWAY

According to legend, this rocky outcrop on the coast of Northern Ireland is an unfinished road built by giants across the Irish Sea to Scotland. In fact, the causeway was formed by volcanic lava that cooled when it met the sea, forming amazing six-sided pillars of rock.

♦ *Northern Ireland's rich soil was created by rock fragments left behind when the glaciers melted.*

Gannets

DECIDUOUS WOODLAND

The warmer parts of northern Europe were once covered in deciduous woodland, but much of it has now been cleared for farms and cities. Deciduous trees such as oak, beech and elm shed their leaves in winter. Squirrels build nests called dreys in the branches of oak trees, and blue tits, woodpeckers and owls live in the upper canopy. On the woodland floor flowers such as bluebells and daffodils come up in spring. Badgers and foxes forage among the leaves for food.

♦ *Badgers sleep in their underground homes, called setts, by day. At dusk they come out to feed on slugs, nuts, berries and voles.*

Oak leaves

Tawny owl

Red fox

Eurasian badger

Hedgehog

Blackbird

Beech leaves

Robin

TRAWLING THE SEAS

The seas around northern Europe are rich in fish such as cod, herring, mackerel and plaice. Iceland's economy depends on fishing, and Denmark is one of the world's biggest exporters. The North Sea and the Atlantic Ocean are often very stormy, and trawling (above) can be a dangerous business.

♦ *Overfishing and pollution have reduced the North Sea's fish stocks, so in Norway, Scotland and Sweden fish are farmed in large tanks.*

LIFE ON THE CLIFFS

Cliffs on the coasts of northern Europe are home to huge colonies of seabirds. Some nesting areas contain tens of thousands of birds. Gannets and cormorants build nests out of seaweed, grass and droppings. Puffins make small burrows on the steep slopes above cliff faces. Many birds return to the same spot year after year to breed.

♦ *Gannets are superb divers. They plunge into the sea from a height of up to 30 m (about 100 ft) to seize fish under water.*

Puffins

Cormorant

HERDING REINDEER

In the very northern parts of Scandinavia, the Sami people herd reindeer as they have done for centuries. The reindeer migrate in huge herds to upland areas to graze in the summer and give birth to calves. As the weather gets cooler, they head for more sheltered woodland areas. Reindeer feed on lichen, moss and grasses.

♦ *The region where the Sami live is sometimes called Lapland. The Sami, or Lapps, have their own language and religion.*

ALBANIA	ANDORRA	AUSTRIA	BELGIUM	BOSNIA-HERZEGOVINA	BULGARIA	CROATIA	CZECH REPUBLIC	FRANCE
Area: 28,748 sq km Population: 3,422,000	Area: 468 sq km Population: 74,839	Area: 83,857 sq km Population: 8,169,000	Area: 30,518 sq km Population: 10,188,000	Area: 51,129 sq km Population: 3,784,000	Area: 110,994 sq km Population: 8,428,000	Area: 56,538 sq km Population: 4,497,000	Area: 78,865 sq km Population: 10,236,000	Area: 543,965 sq km Population: 58,747

East, West and South

Europe
People and places

The countries of Europe have many different cultures and customs, but they also have a lot in common. Greek and Roman civilizations influenced ideas of art, philosophy and law. Christianity is a shared religion. Centuries of trade and industry helped build up great cities such as Rome, Paris and Berlin. In this century, two world wars shattered the continent and the rivalry between capitalist and communist systems of government split it in two. Western European countries founded the European Union to deliver peace and prosperity. Since 1989, when the Cold War between East and West ended, trade and travel across the whole of Europe have increased again.

PARISIAN CAFE

In many European cities, small squares lined with cafés, like this one in the Montmartre district of Paris, are a familiar sight. Coffee was first brought to Paris from the East in 1686, and cafés soon became popular across Europe.

♦ *French culture has enriched the world with its writers, painters, philosophers, film directors and chefs.*

N

Kilometres
0 100 200 300 400 500

0 100 200 300
Miles

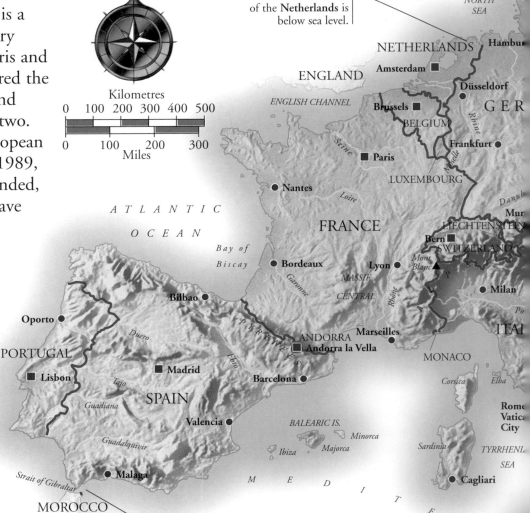

Half of the land area of the **Netherlands** is below sea level.

DENMARK
NORTH SEA
NETHERLANDS
ENGLAND
Amsterdam
Hambur
Düsseldorf
ENGLISH CHANNEL
Brussels
BELGIUM
GER
Rhine
Frankfurt
ATLANTIC OCEAN
Paris
LUXEMBOURG
Nantes
Seine
Loire
Danub
Mur
FRANCE
LIECHTENSTEIN
Bern
SWITZERLAND
Bay of Biscay
Bordeaux
Lyon
Mont Blanc
Milan
Bilbao
MASSIF CENTRAL
Po
Oporto
Duero
Rhône
ITAL
PORTUGAL
ANDORRA
Marseilles
Andorra la Vella
MONACO
Corsica
Elba
Lisbon
Madrid
Tajo
Barcelona
Rome
Vatican City
Guadiana
SPAIN
BALEARIC IS.
Valencia
Minorca
Sardinia
TYRRHENI SEA
Guadalquivir
Ibiza
Majorca
Strait of Gibraltar
Malaga
M E D I
Cagliari
MOROCCO
T E R R

DELPHI

Ancient Greeks went to the Temple of Apollo at Delphi to consult the oracle, an elderly priestess who made prophecies about the future. Now the ruined site (left) attracts thousands of tourists.

♦ *The ancient Greeks had many gods. Apollo was the god of music and poetry.*

BRITTANY

Every year the Breton people of Brittany in France hold an annual festival called the Joining of the Hands (right). It brings together many of the Celtic peoples of Europe, including Scots, Irish, Welsh, Galicians from northern Spain and Manx from the Isle of Man.

♦ *Celts spread across Europe between 800 BC and AD 100.*

Europe and Africa are separated by the **Strait of Gibraltar**, only 14 km (9 mi) wide.

VENETIAN CARNIVAL

The city of Venice, in Italy, is built on over 100 islands in a lagoon. It has 177 canals, which serve as streets. In early spring the Venetians hold a spectacular carnival, in which decorated gondolas are steered by boatmen in fancy costumes.

♦ *Venice is slowly sinking and many buildings are in peril.*

GERMANY Area: 356,955 sq km Population: 82,190,000

GREECE Area: 131,957 sq km Population: 10,522,000

HUNGARY Area: 93,031 sq km Population: 9,989,000

ITALY Area: 301,277 sq km Population: 57,240,000

LIECHTEN- STEIN Area: 160 sq km Population: 28,000

LUXEMBOURG Area: 2,586 sq km Population: 417,000

MACEDONIA Area: 25,713 sq km Population: 2,180,000

MALTA Area: 316 sq km Population: 371,000

MOLDOVA Area: 33,700 sq km Population: 4,448,000

VILLAGE LIFE

In many parts of eastern Europe life remains traditional. People work on small farms, often without machinery, and many homes lack modern comforts. This is a typical Romanian village scene.

♦ More than a third of Romanians are farmers.

PRAGUE

In Prague, capital of the Czech Republic, there are well-preserved buildings from all periods since the Middle Ages. Charlemagne, the first Holy Roman Emperor, was born there. From the 1500s the city was a centre of the Habsburg dynasty, one of Europe's great ruling families. Famous landmarks are the medieval castle on Hradcany hill, the cathedral of St Vitus and the famous Charles Bridge, built across the Vltava river over 600 years ago by Charles IV, King of Bohemia.

♦ Bohemia's patron saint, St Wenceslas (AD 907–929), has an elegant Prague square named after him.

In the ancient woodland of the **Bialowieza National Park** in Poland, there are bison, wolves, otters and beavers.

Ukraine's capital, **Kiev**, dates from the 6th century. Its Grand Prince made Christianity the state religion in 988.

Greece has over 2,000 islands, only 170 of which have people living on them.

NEUSCHWANSTEIN

Europe is full of castles. Many were built for defence, but fairy-tale Neuschwanstein in southern Germany (left), was built by "mad" King Ludwig II as a place to hide away from the world. After being declared mad in 1886, he was found drowned.

♦ Almost every room in Ludwig's castle has a swan in its design.

Data file

Area	3,859,991 sq km/1,490,354 sq mi
Population	478 million
Independent countries	31
Largest country	Ukraine (603,700 sq km/233,100 sq mi)
Smallest country	Vatican City (0.44 sq km/0.17 sq mi)
Most populated country	Germany (82,190,000)
Least populated country	Vatican City (840)
Largest cities	Paris, France (9.3 million); Madrid, Spain (3 million)
Highest mountain	Mont Blanc, France/Italy (4,807 m/15,770 ft)
Longest river	Danube, 6 countries (2,850 km/1,770 mi)
Largest lake	Lake Balaton, Hungary (590 sq km/230 sq mi)
Religions	Roman Catholic, Protestant, Orthodox, Muslim
Languages	National languages

How places got their names

Alps	from the Celtic word for rock or mountain
Mediterranean	from the Latin for sea in the middle of the earth
Paris	from a Celtic tribe called the Parisii
Poland	from the Slavonic for low-lying land
Portugal	from the Latin for warm harbour

MONACO Area: 1.95 sq km Population: 27,000
NETHERLANDS Area: 41,863 sq km Population: 15,683,000
POLAND Area: 312,683 sq km Population: 38,636,000
PORTUGAL Area: 92,389 sq km Population: 9,803,000
ROMANIA Area: 237,500 sq km Population: 22,606,000
SAN MARINO Area: 61 sq km Population: 24,000
SLOVAKIA Area: 49,035 sq km Population: 5,356,000
SLOVENIA Area: 20,251 sq km Population: 1,922,000
SPAIN Area: 504,750 sq km Population: 39,733,000

East, West and South Europe: Nature

Europe is the second smallest continent after Australasia. It lies between the cold Baltic and North Seas to the north and the warm Mediterranean Sea to the south. For such a small region, there is a remarkable variety of landscapes and habitats. A vast lowland plain stretches from the Netherlands to the Ukraine, dotted with marshes, lakes and rivers. In the south, mountain ranges like the Alps, Carpathians and Pyrenees still support wild animals such as lynxes and ibexes. Centuries of human habitation have threatened many wild species, which is why the conservation of wetlands and other areas is now so important.

POSTOGNA CAVES

The limestone rock outcrops of the Balkan Peninsula (between the Adriatic and Aegean Seas) contain many huge cave systems, such as this one in Postogna, Slovenia. Over the course of 2 million years, the river Pivka has hollowed out over 27 km (17 mi) of tunnels. The Concert Hall cave is so big that a symphony orchestra once held a performance inside.

♦ A blind, colourless salamander lives in these caves. Local people used to think it was a baby dragon.

MEDITERRANEAN PLANTS

The Mediterranean has long, hot summers and short, cool winters. Many plants in the region survive the intense heat and drought by flowering only in the spring and autumn. In the summer they die back above ground. But under the soil they have enough food stored in their bulbs to keep them alive until the next growing period. Anemones, irises, fritillaries and cyclamens all grow from bulbs.

♦ Scented herbs such as lavender, rosemary, sage and thyme grow in the Mediterranean.

Anemone

Fritillary

Iris

Cyclamen

CAMARGUE WETLANDS

The Camargue in southern France is one of Europe's most important wetland areas. It covers 800 sq km (300 sq mi) at the mouth of the river Rhône, where it enters the Mediterranean Sea. The landscape is a mix of fresh and salt water, reed beds, woodlands, dunes and lagoons. This varied habitat is home to hundreds of plants, birds and other animals. It is the only European home of the greater flamingo (below). Egrets, bee eaters, hoopoes and marsh harriers also live there. Local farmers keep herds of black bulls in the marshlands.

♦ An ancient breed of beautiful white horses lives wild in the Camargue wetlands.

OCELLATED LIZARD

In the warmer regions of Europe lizards are a familiar sight. They can often be seen basking in the sun on rocks or walls to warm their bodies up. The ocellated lizard (above) belongs to a family of green lizards found throughout the region. It grows up to 20 cm (8 in) long, and is one of the largest European lizards. It likes to live in dry, bushy places.

♦ Lizards regularly shed their skin. The old dead layer peels off to reveal a new one underneath.

SWITZERLAND
Area: 41,293 sq km
Population: 7,277,000

UKRAINE
Area: 603,700 sq km
Population: 51,424,000

VATICAN CITY
Area: 0.44 sq km
Population: 840

YUGOSLAVIA
Area: 25,713 sq km
Population: 10,559,000

Golden eagle

MOUNTAIN LANDSCAPE

For centuries few people lived in the European mountains. Large animals that had been hunted to extinction elsewhere survived there. Brown bears are still found in the Cantabrians in Spain, lynxes live in the Romanian Carpathians and wolves are making a comeback in the Italian Apennines. Other animals, such as ibexes and mouflons, have adapted well to rocky habitats. The ibex is very agile and has special hooves that allow it to land softly when it jumps.

♦ *The small Alpine marmot lives at altitudes of up to 3,200 m (10,500 ft). It sleeps all through the winter, living off reserves of body fat.*

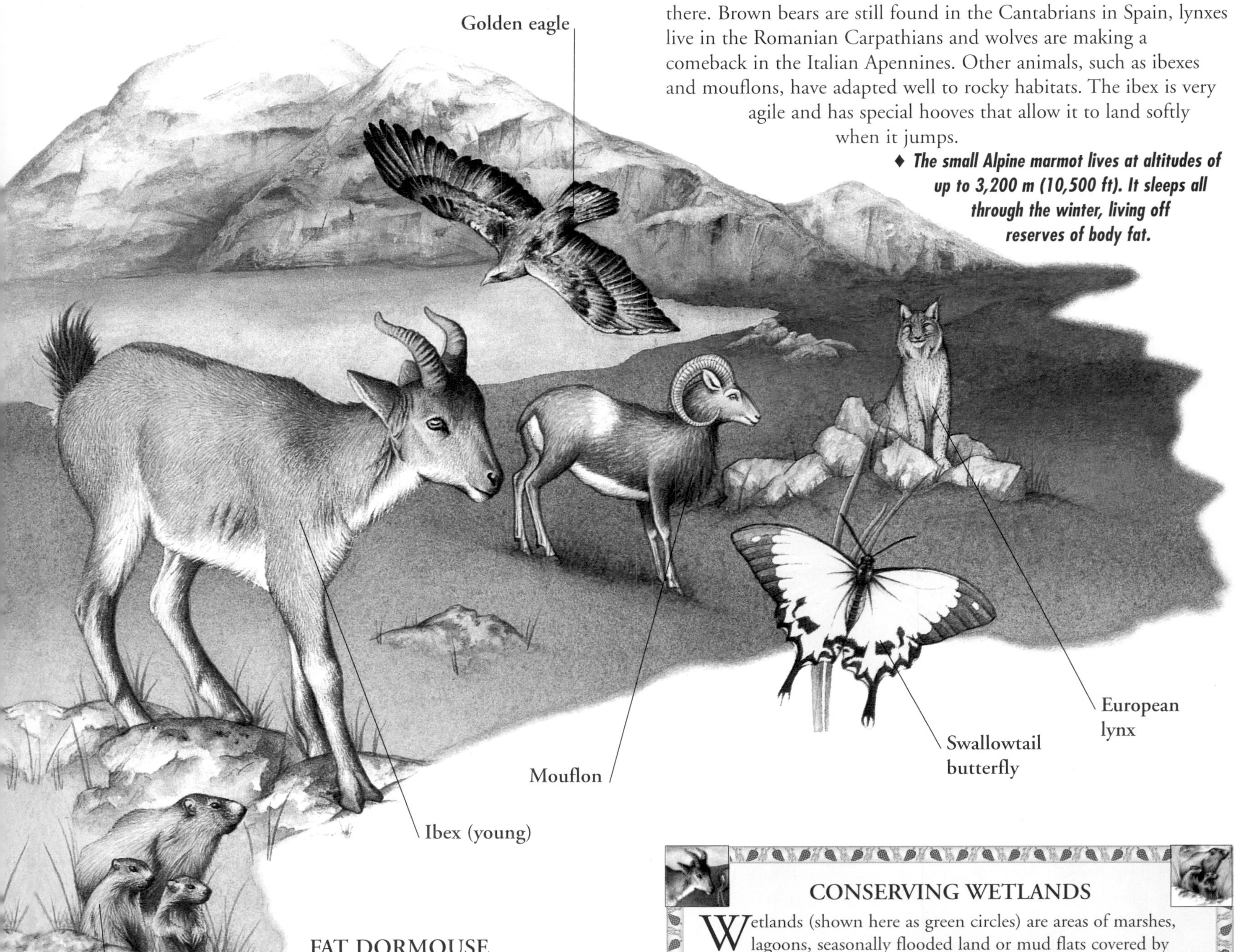

European lynx

Swallowtail butterfly

Mouflon

Ibex (young)

Marmot

FAT DORMOUSE

The fat dormouse (below) is twice as large as a common dormouse. It lives in woodlands, coming out at night to forage in the trees for seeds, nuts and insects to eat. This dormouse has a long, bushy tail that helps it balance as it moves from branch to branch. It makes a nest out of moss and leaves in a hollow tree. Sometimes dormice are found living in the roof spaces of houses.

♦ *The ancient Romans prized fat dormice as a great food delicacy. They kept them in wooden enclosures and fattened them with fruit and nuts.*

CONSERVING WETLANDS

Wetlands (shown here as green circles) are areas of marshes, lagoons, seasonally flooded land or mud flats covered by tidal waters. They are important habitats for many wild animals, migrating birds, fish and other water creatures. Throughout Europe, wetland areas are under threat. Farmers drain the land to make fields, and often chemicals used in farming and industry find their way into the water. Protecting Europe's wetlands is very important for preserving its wildlife.

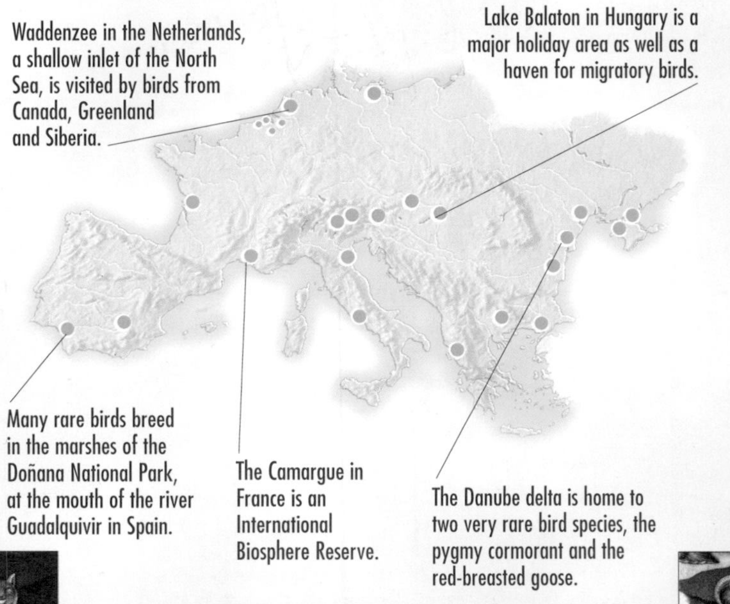

Waddenzee in the Netherlands, a shallow inlet of the North Sea, is visited by birds from Canada, Greenland and Siberia.

Lake Balaton in Hungary is a major holiday area as well as a haven for migratory birds.

Many rare birds breed in the marshes of the Doñana National Park, at the mouth of the river Guadalquivir in Spain.

The Camargue in France is an International Biosphere Reserve.

The Danube delta is home to two very rare bird species, the pygmy cormorant and the red-breasted goose.

East, West and South Europe:
Farming and industry

Europe has been a major centre for trade for centuries. It is a region rich in natural resources, such as fertile farmland, water, coal and iron ore. Europe's colonies overseas provided more resources and markets for its nations' goods. Germany, France and Italy are among the world's leading industrial nations, while smaller countries such as Switzerland and Luxembourg are centres of banking and finance. But there are still many rural areas, especially in the east, where traditional ways of life based on farming continue to be practised.

FARMING IN POLAND

In many east European countries, like Poland and Romania, many farmers cannot afford tractors or modern pesticides and fertilizers. They use horses and oxen for ploughing, and harvest hay and crops by hand, as these Polish farmers near Zakopane (above) are doing. The hay — cut and dried grass — is used to feed farm animals in the winter when there is nothing for them to graze on.

♦ *Poland's main crops are wheat, barley, rye and potatoes.*

SUPERCAR

Europeans were among the earliest inventors and makers of petrol-driven cars. Among them were Karl Benz, Armand Peugeot and Louis Renault, whose names still appear on cars today. Among the most expensive cars are Italian Ferraris (left). The firm was founded by the racing-car driver Enzo Ferrari in 1939.

♦ *Europe's biggest producers of passenger cars are Germany, France, Spain and Italy.*

DUTCH WINDMILL

Before the invention of the steam engine in the 1700s, windmills were used across much of western Europe for grinding grain into flour. The sails turned grindstones that crushed the grain. In low-lying regions such as the Netherlands, windmills were also used to pump water from flooded fields (below). Nowadays more advanced technology is used, but old windmills are a common sight across the landscape.

♦ *Half of the available land in the Netherlands is used for farming.*

ROTTERDAM

The port of Rotterdam (above), on the mouth of the river Rhine in the Netherlands, handles more cargo than any other port in the world. Over 40 percent of Europe's ship-carried imports from the United States arrive in Rotterdam, and much of the continent's crude oil is delivered to its oil refineries and chemical works. Other goods arrive in large, standard-size containers that can be quickly and easily transferred to trucks or smaller cargo boats. These boats can travel to much of Europe's industrial heartland along rivers and canals.

♦ *Rotterdam is 30 km (19 mi) from the North Sea. Ships reach it via the New Waterway, built by the Dutch in 1872.*

SUNFLOWERS

In parts of Europe where the climate is hot and dry, such as the Spanish region of Andalusia (below), sunflowers and fruit such as oranges are ideally suited to the dry conditions. Here, temperatures reach 29° C (84° F) in summer and the winters are cool. Sunflowers are grown commercially for a range of products: the leaves make fodder for animals, and the seeds can be crushed to produce oil, which goes into soap and paint or can be used for cooking. The seeds can also be roasted and eaten by themselves. Sunflowers also make popular garden plants, growing as high as 5 m (16 ft).

♦ *Sunflowers come from North America and were brought to Spain in the 1500s. They get their name because their heads turn to follow the sun.*

NUCLEAR POWER

France has only small reserves of coal and gas and no oilfields, so the French government decided to use nuclear power to meet the country's energy needs. France started its first reactor in 1959. Nuclear power now provides about 75 percent of the country's electricity. These workers at La Hague (above) are constructing cells for the nuclear reactor. Inside the reactor core, atoms of plutonium or uranium are split, releasing tremendous energy. This is known as nuclear fission. The energy heats up water into steam, which is then used to turn turbines and generate electricity.

♦ *Nuclear power stations need a lot of water to cool the reactor and make steam, so most are on coasts or beside rivers.*

RHINE BARGE

The river Rhine rises in the Swiss Alps and flows to the North Sea, passing through Germany and the Netherlands. Other rivers and canals join the Rhine, including a canal which links it to the river Danube. This means that barges can travel from the North Sea to the Black Sea. These waterways were very important in Europe's early industrial revolution, and still are today. Special boats called pusher barges (left) are used to move big loads. They can shift heavier cargoes than vessels that pull their loads.

♦ *Because the Rhine is so important to European trade, it has been treated as an international waterway since 1815.*

BELARUS	GEORGIA	KAZAKH-STAN	KYRGYZ-STAN	RUSSIA	TAJIK-ISTAN	TURKMEN-ISTAN	UZBEK-ISTAN
Area: 207,600 sq km Population: 10,338,000	Area: 69,700 sq km Population: 5,435,000	Area: 2,717,300 sq km Population: 16,832,000	Area: 198,500 sq km Population: 4,480,000	Area: 17,075,400 sq km Population: 147,709,000	Area: 143,100 sq km Population: 6,045,000	Area: 488,100 sq km Population: 4,235,000	Area: 447,400 sq km Population: 23,656,000

Russia
and its neighbours
People and places

Russia is the world's largest country. It is so big that you cross 11 time zones when you travel its whole width. While people are having breakfast in the west, in the east they are having their evening meal. This vast region, which includes the mainly Muslim countries of central Asia and the small countries around the Caucasus Mountains, was once ruled by the Russian empire and then, from 1922 to 1991, by the Communist-run Union of Soviet Socialist Republics (USSR). Since 1991, the former Soviet bloc countries neighbouring Russia have gained independence.

RUSSIAN PRIESTS

These priests belong to the Russian Orthodox Church. Russian Orthodoxy was heavily suppressed by the Communist government of the USSR, but after Communism collapsed in 1991 the Russian people were allowed to go to church again, and Moscow's main cathedral was rebuilt.

♦ *The Russian Orthodox Church has its own calendar. It celebrates Christmas 13 days after most other Christian countries.*

ST BASIL'S CATHEDRAL

The Cathedral of St Basil the Blessed stands next to Red Square in Moscow. It was built by Ivan the Terrible in the 16th century, in thanks for his victories over the Tartars, which enabled him to expand the Russian empire eastwards.

♦ *The cathedral was badly damaged by Napoleon's army in 1812.*

In summer timber is exported from the port of **Arkhangel'sk**, but in winter the port is iced up.

The first manned space rocket took off in 1961 from **Baikonur**, Kazakhstan, where the Russian space programme is based.

SOVIET SOUVENIRS

This man is selling old Soviet army hats in a busy shopping district of Moscow. Young Russian men had to serve in the armed forces, but after the fall of Communism many soldiers found themselves unpaid and without a job. Selling army goods is one way to make a living.

♦ *In Moscow it is common to see people selling wild mushrooms they have collected in the woods near the city.*

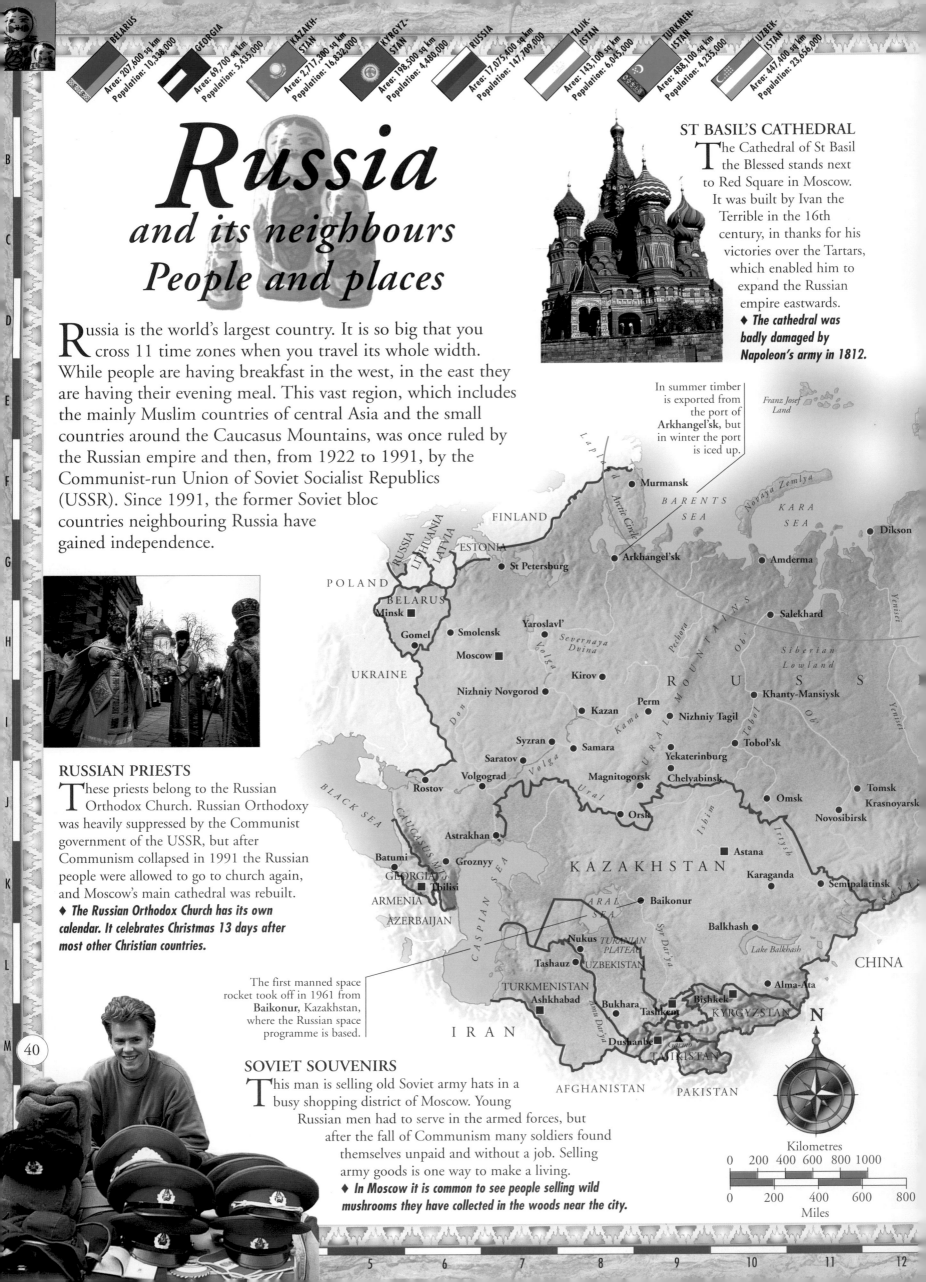

Kilometres
0 200 400 600 800 1000

0 200 400 600 800
Miles

MIR SPACE STATION

In 1971 the Soviet Union launched the first space station to orbit the Earth. In 1986 space station Mir (right) was launched and manned by a crew of cosmonauts.

♦ **US space shuttles regularly visited Mir from 1995 to 1998.**

TRADITIONAL RUSSIA

Many Russian foods use grains and vegetables grown on the country's rich soils. Black rye bread is a staple, and small pancakes called blinis are served with the most prized delicacy, caviar — the tiny black eggs of the sturgeon fish. Soup is often eaten at lunchtime; a favourite is beetroot soup, called borscht, served with sour cream. Water for tea is heated in an urn called a samovar.

♦ **The balalaika is a Russian musical instrument invented in the 18th century, and Russian dolls are a traditional toy.**

Borscht soup

Tea

Blinis with caviar

Russian dolls

Black rye bread

Balalaika

Samovar

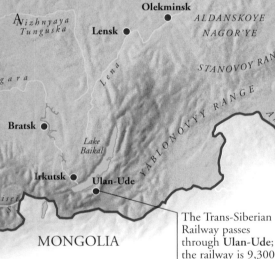

Verkhoyansk is the coldest city in the world: a temperature of -71°C (-95°F) has been recorded.

Kamchatka has 22 active volcanoes. The largest is Klyuchevskaya.

Bering St.

BERING SEA

Anadyr'

Os. Vrangelya

Arctic Circle

ARCTIC OCEAN

EAST SIBERIAN SEA

Novosibirskiye Ostrova

Os. Lyakhovskiy

LAPTEV SEA

Delta of the Lena

vernaya Zemlya

Nordvik

CENTRAL SIBERIAN PLATEAU

Indigirka

CHERSKOGO RANGE

VERKHOYANSK RANGE

Verkhoyansk

Kolyma

Kolyma Lowland

KOLYMA RANGE

Magadan

▲ *Klyuchevskaya*

KAMCHATKA

SEA OF OKHOTSK

Yakutsk

Lena

Olekminsk

ALDANSKOYE NAGOR'YE

DZHUGDZHUR RANGE

Sakhalin

Lensk

Nizhnyaya Tunguska

STANOVOY RANGE

YABLONOVYY RANGE

Amur

Tatarskiy Proliv

SIKHOTE ALIN

Bratsk

Lake Baikal

Kharbarovsk

Irkutsk

Ulan-Ude

nisei

TS

ngara

MONGOLIA

The Trans-Siberian Railway passes through **Ulan-Ude**; the railway is 9,300 km (5,780 mi) long.

Vladivostok

SAMARKAND

Many people have conquered this ancient city in Uzbekistan, including Persians, Greeks, Arabs, Turks and Russians. It was the capital of Tamerlane, a warrior emperor who ruled the Mongols from 1369 to 1405. Around Registan Square (right) in the old city there are three madrasahs, or Islamic schools.

♦ **Tamerlane's armies rampaged across central Asia, all the way from India to Turkey.**

ST PETERSBURG

Russia's second largest city was planned by Tsar Peter I in 1703. He wanted a capital closer to the rest of Europe than Moscow. The city has many fine buildings, including the Hermitage Museum (left) in the Tsar's Winter Palace.

♦ **St Petersburg was called Petrograd and then Leningrad under the Soviet Union.**

Data file

Area	21,347,100 sq km/8,242,179 sq mi
Population	219 million
Independent countries	8
Largest country	Russia (17,075,400 sq km/6,592,800 sq mi)
Smallest country	Georgia (69,700 sq km/26,900 sq mi)
Most populated country	Russia (147,709,000)
Least populated country	Turkmenistan (4,235,000)
Largest cities	Moscow, Russia (8.7 million); St Petersburg, Russia (4.8 million)
Highest mountain	Garmo (Communism Peak), Tajikistan (7,495 m/24,590 ft)
Longest rivers	Yenisei (5,870 km/3,650 mi); Ob-Irtysh (5,411 km/3,362 mi)
Largest lakes	Caspian Sea (370,992 sq km/143,241 sq mi); Aral Sea (37,000 sq km/14,290 sq mi)
Religions	Russian Orthodox, Muslim
Languages	Russian, national languages

Russia and its neighbours:
Nature, farming and industry

The natural landscapes of this region are strongly influenced by climate. They are arranged in huge bands stretching west to east. In the Arctic north, winters are bitterly cold and the soil is permanently frozen. Reindeer herders live there. To the south of this cold zone there are vast coniferous forests, called taiga, where bears and sable live. Then there are the wide grasslands called steppes, which are home to herds of grazing animals. Further south are dry lands and deserts, surrounding the inland waters of the Caspian and Aral Seas. Most Russians live in the European part of the region to the west of the Ural Mountains. Here the richer soils make good farmland and the climate is less severe. Industries based on iron and coal grew around the Volga and Don river basins.

STREET MARKET
People in this part of the world like to buy their fresh fruit and vegetables from open-air markets like this one (above). The traders are often from small family farms. They come to the city each day to sell their produce. City people also grow their own food in small plots next to their wooden summer houses in the countryside, called dachas.
♦ *Under Communist rule, farmers had to work on large, state-owned farms.*

HERDERS OF THE NORTH
The northern parts of Russia are too cold to grow crops. So many people of the region, such as the Buryats, Yakuts and Nentsi, make their living by herding reindeer or catching fish. They eat reindeer meat and make clothes from the animals' skins. This man (right) is from the Taz River region of western Siberia.
♦ *Siberia is rich in oil, natural gas, coal, iron and gold. Although these resources have been developed, local people have been allowed to carry on a traditional way of life.*

SHRINKING SEA
The Aral Sea (left) lies between Uzbekistan and Kazakhstan, but it is fed by waters from Tajikistan, Kyrgyzstan and Afghanistan. These countries are very dry, so they quarrel over scarce water. So much water has been taken from the rivers to irrigate cotton fields that in recent years the sea has shrunk drastically.
♦ *The Aral Sea's water level has fallen by 16 m (53 ft) over the last 30 years, leaving ships stranded and rusting on the former lake bed.*

ON THE STEPPES
The steppes form a vast plain that stretches all the way from Ukraine to Siberia. These sweeping grasslands are bordered by woods to the north and by desert to the south. The climate is generally too cold in winter and too hot and dry in summer for trees to survive. But grasses such as feather grass and needle grass have deep roots that can tap water from under the ground. This helps them withstand the drought.
♦ *The saiga lives on the steppes. Its large nose has hair-lined passages to warm up the air and filter out dust.*

Hamster

Saiga

Sandgrouse

Great bustard

Feather grass

OIL PIPELINE

Huge oil reserves have been found in western Siberia, in the Ural-Volga region and around the Caspian Sea. To get the oil to distant cities, long pipelines have had to be laid (right), often in remote places and under very difficult wintry conditions.

♦ **Russia has 63,000 km (39,000 mi) of oil pipelines.**

FARMING REGIONS

Although this is a vast region, much of the land is not good for farming. The north is too cold, the south too hot and other regions are too far from markets and consumers. The best farmland is where woodlands have been cleared. This has produced chernozem, or black earth, which supports big wheat fields. In desert regions, irrigation makes it possible to grow cotton and rice.

Many farms in western Russia specialize in cabbages and root crops.

Around Moscow is an area of market gardening.

In the far east it is hot and rainy enough to grow vegetables, rice and fruit.

The dry lands of Central Asia are suited to herds of sheep, goats, camels and horses.

River water is diverted from the Aral Sea to irrigate cotton fields.

	Reindeer
	Dairy
	Grain, crops & livestock
	Sheep, goats & camels
	Fruit
	Cotton

Osprey

Sable

Baikal seal

CHANGING WAYS

Under the Communist system, the government of the Soviet Union ran most factories and farms. This meant that people's basic needs of food, clothing and housing were met, and rents were low. But luxuries, especially from abroad, were almost impossible to come by. When the US fast-food chain McDonald's opened its first restaurant in Moscow in 1990, people queued for hours to get in.

♦ **Under its last Communist leader, Mikhail Gorbachev, the government started to allow more foreign companies to invest in the country.**

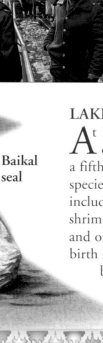

LAKE BAIKAL

At 1,620 m (5,315 ft), Lake Baikal is the deepest lake in the world, and it contains a fifth of all the world's fresh water. Many species are found nowhere else in the world, including 52 kinds of fish and 250 different shrimps. The Baikal seal is the world's smallest and only freshwater seal. The females give birth in early spring, in solitary lairs under breathing holes in the snow.

♦ **Lake Baikal has 336 rivers flowing into it, but just one outlet, the River Angara.**

ARMENIA
Area: 29,800 sq km
Population: 3,642,000

AZERBAIJAN
Area: 86,600 sq km
Population: 7,655,000

BAHRAIN
Area: 691 sq km
Population: 582,000

CYPRUS
Area: 9,251 sq km
Population: 767,000

IRAN
Area: 1,643,503 sq km
Population: 71,518,000

IRAQ
Area: 438,317 sq km
Population: 21,177,000

ISRAEL
Area: 20,700 sq km
Population: 5,781,000

JORDAN
Area: 89,206 sq km
Population: 5,774,000

KUWAIT
Area: 17,818 sq km
Population: 1,731,000

South West Asia
People and places

South West Asia, also often called the Middle East, lies at the junction of three continents: Africa, Asia and Europe. This region has been very important throughout history. Ancient cultures such as the Sumerian and Persian civilizations thrived in the area between the Tigris and Euphrates rivers, called Mesopotamia. They developed writing about 4000 BC and the plough about 3500 BC. Later, the great world religions of Judaism, Christianity and Islam began in the region. Today, Jerusalem and Mecca are major centres of pilgrimage and worship. For centuries, nomads have herded animals across the dry lands, but increasingly people from rural areas are moving to the region's thriving modern cities, such as Istanbul and Tehran.

TRADITIONAL CURE

This Turkish woman (right) is having a traditional treatment for arthritis. Her inflamed joints are soothed by the effects of being buried in sand. The leaves protect her head from the heat of the sun.

♦ *Turkey is a rapidly developing country with free health care for the poor, but many traditional ways live on.*

The bridges across the Bosporus Strait in **Istanbul** connect Europe with Asia.

BEDOUIN NOMADS

The Bedouin are traditionally nomadic and are known as a proud and independent people. They used to trade across deserts, moving their herds of sheep, goats and cattle from one sparse pasture to another. But their most prized animal is the camel, which provides milk and meat and can carry heavy loads. Camels have been known to go for many months without water.

♦ *There are about one million Bedouin in South West Asia. Many have settled as farmers.*

PETRA

The ancient city of Petra in Jordan was carved out of sandstone rock in about 1000 BC by the Edomites. In 312 BC it became the capital of the Nabateans, who were Arab nomads. After an earthquake in AD 551, the city was deserted and left in ruins. All that remains are striking facades cut into the rock and numerous cave dwellings.

♦ *Petra is approached through a narrow passage between cliffs. It was rediscovered in 1812 by a Swiss traveller disguised as an Arab.*

MECCA

The prophet Mohammed was born in Mecca, now in Saudi Arabia, in AD 570. Mecca is one of Islam's holiest places, and every year two million worshippers travel to the Great Mosque (right) on a pilgrimage called the hajj.

♦ *There are more than one thousand million Muslims worldwide.*

WOMEN'S DRESS

In many parts of the region, it is the custom for women to be fully covered and to reveal their faces only to relatives. This Iranian woman is wearing a dress called a chador.

♦ **Bedouin women wear traditional robes and a black mask or veil.**

WAILING WALL

Jerusalem is a holy city for Muslims, Jews and Christians. The Wailing Wall (right) is all that remains of the Temple of King Herod, destroyed in AD 70 by the Romans. It is one of the Jews' holiest sites, where people go to pray and leave written messages to God in the crevices of the wall.

♦ **The golden Dome of the Rock behind the Wailing Wall is a holy place for Muslims.**

Iran was once ruled by the powerful Persian empire, founded in 550 BC by Cyrus the Great.

CEREMONIAL DAGGER

Some men in Oman and Yemen still carry a ceremonial dagger, called a khanjar, as a sign of their importance. The finest daggers have scabbards inlaid with silver and handles made of ivory, whalebone or rhinoceros horn.

♦ **When Omani women marry, they are traditionally given a beautiful silver necklace called a labba.**

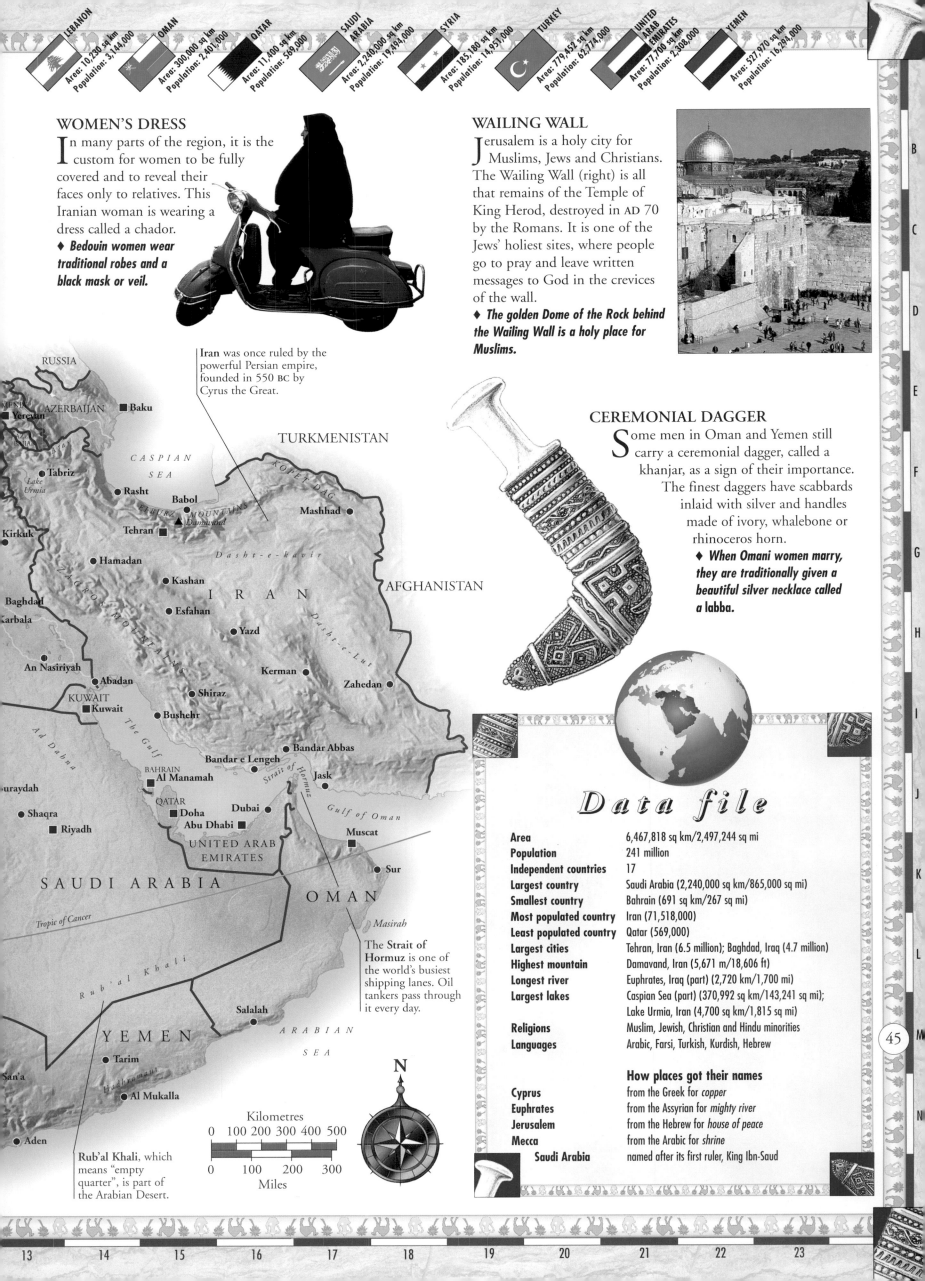

RUSSIA
AZERBAIJAN
Baku
Yerevan
Tabriz
Lake Urmia
CASPIAN SEA
Rasht
Babol
TURKMENISTAN
KOPET DAG
Mashhad
ELBURZ MOUNTAINS
Damavand
Tehran
Hamadan
Dasht-e-kavir
Kirkuk
Kashan
I R A N
AFGHANISTAN
Baghdad
Esfahan
Karbala
Yazd
ZAGROS MOUNTAINS
Dasht-e-Lut
An Nasiriyah
Kerman
Abadan
Shiraz
Zahedan
KUWAIT
Kuwait
Bushehr
Ad Dahna
The Gulf
Bandar Abbas
Bandar e Lengeh
BAHRAIN
Al Manamah
Strait of Hormuz
Jask
uraydah
QATAR
Dubai
Gulf of Oman
Shaqra
Doha
Abu Dhabi
Riyadh
UNITED ARAB EMIRATES
Muscat
SAUDI ARABIA
O M A N
Sur
Tropic of Cancer
Masirah

The **Strait of Hormuz** is one of the world's busiest shipping lanes. Oil tankers pass through it every day.

Rub'al Khali
Salalah
Y E M E N
ARABIAN SEA
San'a
Tarim
Hadhramaut
Al Mukalla
Aden

Rub'al Khali, which means "empty quarter", is part of the Arabian Desert.

Kilometres
0 100 200 300 400 500

0 100 200 300
Miles

N

Data file

Area	6,467,818 sq km/2,497,244 sq mi
Population	241 million
Independent countries	17
Largest country	Saudi Arabia (2,240,000 sq km/865,000 sq mi)
Smallest country	Bahrain (691 sq km/267 sq mi)
Most populated country	Iran (71,518,000)
Least populated country	Qatar (569,000)
Largest cities	Tehran, Iran (6.5 million); Baghdad, Iraq (4.7 million)
Highest mountain	Damavand, Iran (5,671 m/18,606 ft)
Longest river	Euphrates, Iraq (part) (2,720 km/1,700 mi)
Largest lakes	Caspian Sea (part) (370,992 sq km/143,241 sq mi); Lake Urmia, Iran (4,700 sq km/1,815 sq mi)
Religions	Muslim, Jewish, Christian and Hindu minorities
Languages	Arabic, Farsi, Turkish, Kurdish, Hebrew

How places got their names

Cyprus	from the Greek for copper
Euphrates	from the Assyrian for mighty river
Jerusalem	from the Hebrew for house of peace
Mecca	from the Arabic for shrine
Saudi Arabia	named after its first ruler, King Ibn-Saud

South West Asia:
Nature, farming and industry

South West Asia is a region dominated by mountains and deserts. Animals and plants have adapted to these harsh environments by making the best of the scarce water. Down the centuries, people have also learned to adapt, sinking wells to reach underground water and building canals to irrigate the land. Along the Gulf coast there are many desalination plants, where salty seawater is treated and turned into fresh water for drinking. In other places, new irrigation methods have brought desert areas to life. In more recent times, oil has joined water as a vital resource to humans. It has brought enormous wealth to countries such as Saudi Arabia, Kuwait, Bahrain, Qatar and the United Arab Emirates.

WILD FLOWERS

The ancient Babylonians and Assyrians were famed for their gardens, which were full of ornamental plants, palms and ponds. The Hanging Gardens of Babylon were one of the Seven Wonders of the Ancient World. Flowers such as the lily, lotus and rose were prized. Popular garden plants of today originally from South West Asia include irises, crocuses and tulips (above: left, centre and right).

♦ **Turkey exports flower bulbs around the world, but protects its rare flowers in woodland reserves.**

HERDING GOATS

Where the land is too dry for planting crops, people graze animals such as sheep, goats and cattle. These animals were first domesticated in South West Asia over 7,000 years ago. This Kurdish goatherd (right) is watching over his animals in eastern Turkey.

♦ **In Turkey and Iran there are more sheep and goats than people.**

Scorpion

Jerboa

DATE PALM

Date palms are ideally suited to dry conditions; their long roots tap water deep underground. After the dates have been picked, they are dried and packed for export abroad. Local people use the trunk and leaves of the date palm for building and furniture.

♦ **Iran, Saudi Arabia and Iraq together produce almost half the world's dates.**

Einkorn   Emmer   Chickpea   Grapevine

REGIONAL CROPS

About 8000 BC in Sumeria, in what is now Iraq, humans first started to plant crops from seeds and store grain after harvests. In this way, agriculture was born.

♦ **All the world's different varieties of wheat originally came from ancient grasses such as einkorn and emmer.**

OILFIELDS

South West Asia is the most important region in the world for oil. About 60 percent of all the world's crude oil is found there. Oil comes from the remains of sea animals buried and crushed in layers of rock and sand over 500 million years ago. People first used oil, which they found in places where it surfaces naturally, for sealing ships' hulls to make them watertight. In the 20th century, drills were invented that could reach and tap oil a very long way below the surface. Usually oil reserves are found at least 150 m (490 ft) down, and they are often found together with natural gas. Sometimes the gas is burned off, producing flares like these (left).

♦ **Saudi Arabia produces 13 percent of the world's crude oil and is the world's biggest oil-producing country. The much smaller United Arab Emirates is also a huge oil producer.**

ARABIAN ORYX

This species of long-horned antelope was once found throughout the deserts of Arabia, including the Empty Quarter of Saudi Arabia, but it died out in its natural habitat in 1972. Fortunately some Arabian oryx were kept in zoos, and these animals were reintroduced to the Omani desert about ten years later.

♦ **The oryx's pale coat helps reflect the heat, and its splayed hooves allow it to walk easily on sand.**

Sinai leopard

Dung beetle

LIFE AMONG THE DUNES

The region's deserts include some of the most inhospitable places on Earth. The Empty Quarter in Saudi Arabia is a sea of sand dunes, with scorching heat and hardly any rainfall. There are also scrub deserts, with dry, rock-strewn ground and a few bushes. Deserts appear empty of life by day, but at night sand cats, the rare Sinai leopard, jerboas and scorpions come out to look for food. Oases are fertile patches in the desert where water reaches the surface.

♦ **Scorpions are hunters with powerful, pincer-like claws and stings in their tails. The mother scorpion carries her tiny young on her back.**

FARMING IN ISRAEL

Israel has only small areas of fertile land. In the Negev Desert (above), people are careful with every drop of water. Farmers lay plastic tubes across fields to deliver water directly to the roots of each plant. They grow vegetables under plastic sheets in winter.

♦ **Israel produces over 90 percent of the food it needs with its efficient farming techniques. It also exports oranges, grapefruit and lemons.**

Southern *Asia*
People and places

There is enormous variety in the religious beliefs, customs, diet, dress and languages of the people of Southern Asia. Some 70 percent of the population live in the countryside, following a traditional way of life. There are nomadic herders in the mountains, farming villages on the plains and fishing communities on the coasts. Fast-growing cities such as Bombay, Karachi and Dhaka are home to millions of people. Religion plays an important part in people's lives. Afghanistan, Bangladesh and Pakistan are primarily Muslim countries, while Bhutan is Buddhist. Nepal has both Hindus and Buddhists, and in India there are Hindus, Muslims, Sikhs, Christians, Buddhists and Jains.

STREET BUSINESS

Towns throughout the region typically include an old quarter of narrow streets and alleys, filled with houses, shops and workshops. People often work from their homes, like this dentist in Peshawar, Pakistan (right), or they run small businesses from street stalls. Crowds of people, cars, bicycle rickshaws, dogs and other animals fill the streets.
♦ *Peshawar is in Pakistan's northwest frontier region, at the foot of the Khyber Pass.*

TEMPLE OFFERINGS

India is famous for its many spectacular temples. At a Jain temple in a small town in India, these Jain priests (right) are making an offering to the giant statue of their saint, Bahubali. Jains will harm no living thing, even insects. Hindus have household shrines where they pray daily, as well as many roadside shrines and temples. Offerings to their gods include coloured powders, rice, flowers and incense.
♦ *Many Hindus go on a pilgrimage to the holy city of Varanasi on the Ganges.*

HOLY MAN

Four out of every five Indians follow the Hindu religion. Hindus believe that the souls of living things never die, but are always reborn. Good deeds may be rewarded and bad deeds punished in the next life. Wandering holy men, called sadhus (right), meditate and live simple lives.
♦ *A sadhu lives with few belongings – a simple garment, staff, begging bowl and water pot.*

BUDDHA'S SACRED TOOTH

Every year the Sri Lankan town of Kandy holds a festival and a great procession. A tooth believed to be from Siddhartha Gautama, the Buddha, is taken from its shrine and carried through the streets by elephant.
♦ *Siddhartha was the Indian prince and spiritual teacher who founded Buddhism.*

GOLDEN TEMPLE

Guru Nanak founded the Sikh religion in the 15th century. There are now about 20 million Sikhs, mostly in northern India but also in communities around the world. The Golden Temple at Amritsar, in the Punjab region of India (below), is the holiest Sikh shrine.
♦ *Sikh men traditionally do not cut their hair and they wear a turban.*

TURKMENISTAN
Mazar-e Sharif
Herat
HINDU KUSH
AFGHANISTAN
Kabul
IRAN
Peshawar
Kandahar
Quetta
Faisalabad
Multan
SULAIMAN RANGE
Bahawalpur
Sutlej
PAKISTAN
Indus
Sukkur
Lake Manchhar
Thar Desert
Karachi
Hyderabad
Jodhpur
Gulf of Kachch
Ahmadabad
Jamnagar
Vadodara
Bhavnagar
Surat
Gulf of Khambhat
Bombay
Pune
Solapur
WESTERN
Kolhapur
Hubli-Dharwa
Mangalore
Mysor
GHATS
Coimbatore
Cochin
Trivandrum
Cape Comorin
INDIAN OCEAN
MALDIVES

TAJ MAHAL

The beautiful Taj Mahal stands in the Indian city of Agra, on the banks of the Yamuna river. It was built by the Mogul emperor, Shah Jahan, as a tomb for his wife. Started in about 1630, it took 20,000 workers 20 years to complete. They created a gleaming, white marble building of perfect proportions, topped by a magnificent dome and surrounded by four tall, narrow minarets. Skilled craftsmen carved intricate designs on the surface of the building. Others laid out gardens and a narrow pool, which reflects the dome in its waters. Shah Jahan was buried beside his wife inside the monument he left to the world.

♦ *The Mogul emperors were Muslims who ruled India from 1526 to 1858.*

TAJIKISTAN

DYE STALL

Indians use natural dyes to colour clothes, prepare foods and make coloured water and powders for festivals. This man is selling dyes in a market in southern India.

♦ *The root of the madder plant gives red dye, and yellow saffron comes from the crocus flower.*

SHERPAS

The Sherpas are farmers, herders and traders who live in the mountains of Nepal. When Europeans and others started climbing the Himalayan peaks, Sherpas were employed by the expeditions as skilled mountaineers, guides and bearers capable of carrying heavy loads.

♦ *Sherpas live in some of the highest villages in the world.*

Srinagar
Lahore
New Delhi
Jaipur
Agra
Lucknow
Kanpur
Allahabad
Varanasi
Patna

Thimphu, the capital of Bhutan, lies high in the Himalayas at 2,450 m (8,038 ft).

CHINA
NEPAL
Annapurna
Mt. Everest
Kathmandu
Thimphu
BHUTAN
Gauhati
Brahmaputra
NAGA HILLS
MYANMAR

Tropic of Cancer
Ghagara
Ganges
Son
Narmada

BANGLADESH
Dhaka
Imphal

Jamshedpur
Calcutta
Chittagong

INDIA
Nagpur
Raipur
Mahanadi

Mouths of the Ganges

DECCAN
Godavari
Cuttack

BAY OF BENGAL

Hyderabad
Vishakhapatnam
EASTERN GHATS
Vijayawada
Krishna
Kurnool

Silt carried by the **Ganges** and **Brahmaputra** rivers creates fertile farmland around the Bay of Bengal.

The **Deccan** plateau in southern central India was formed by a giant sheet of volcanic lava.

Nellore
Bangalore
Madras

Tiruchchirappalli
adurai
Jaffna
Gulf of Mannar

SRI LANKA
Kandy
Colombo
Galle
Trincomalee

N

ANDAMAN IS.
Andaman Sea
NICOBAR IS.
Gt. Nicobar

Kilometres
0 100 200 300 400 500

0 100 200 300
Miles

Data file

Area	5,139,660 sq km/1,984,438 sq mi
Population	1,291 million
Independent countries	8
Largest country	India (3,287,263 sq km/1,269,219 sq mi)
Smallest country	Maldives (288 sq km/115 sq mi)
Most populated country	India (960,178,000)
Least populated country	Maldives (273,000)
Largest cities	Bombay, India (12.6 million); Calcutta, India (11 million)
Highest mountain	Mount Everest, Nepal/China (8,848 m/29,028 ft)
Longest river	Indus, Pakistan (2,900 km/1,800 mi)
Largest lake	Manchhar, Pakistan (260 sq km/100 sq mi)
Religions	Hindu, Muslim, Buddhist
Languages	Hindi, English, Bengali, Marathi, Gujarati, Assamese, Punjabi, Urdu, Pashto, Nepali, Dzongkha, Sinhala

How places got their names

Mount Everest	after Sir George Everest (1790–1866), surveyor-general of India
Himalayas	from the Sanskrit for *abode of the snow*

Southern Asia:
Nature

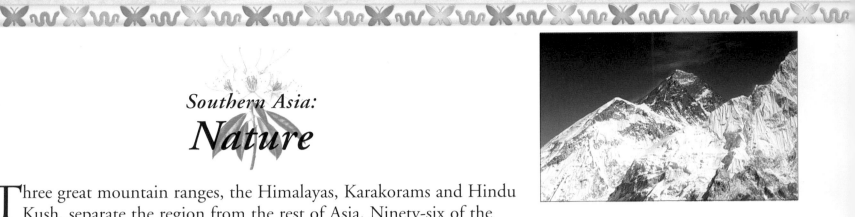

Three great mountain ranges, the Himalayas, Karakorams and Hindu Kush, separate the region from the rest of Asia. Ninety-six of the world's tallest peaks, including the highest of all, Mount Everest, are found here. Melting snow in the highlands feeds huge rivers such as the Indus, Ganges and Brahmaputra. Some of the world's first cities and civilizations were built on the lower plains beside their waters. The area where the Ganges and Brahmaputra rivers enter the Indian Ocean is a low-lying delta region of shifting river channels and mangrove swamps. Central India was once covered in tropical forests, which were home to elephants, tigers and monkeys. Today, much of the forest has been cleared to make way for farmland.

MOUNT EVEREST

The highest mountain peak in the world, Mount Everest, is over 8 km (4.9 mi) above sea level. Everest lies on the border between Nepal and Tibet (China). The first people to conquer the steep, icy slopes and rapidly changing weather of the higher peaks and reach the summit were a New Zealander, Edmund Hillary, and a Nepali Sherpa, Tenzing Norgay, in 1953.
♦ *The mountain's Tibetan name is Chomolungma, meaning "mother goddess of the earth".*

Snow leopard   Himalayan tahr   Lammergeier

Marmot

MOUNTAIN WILDLIFE

Many different animals live in the forests of the Himalayan foothills. Others, such as the goat-like Himalayan tahr, survive on the rocky slopes above the trees, feeding on vegetation among the rocks. The magnificent snow leopard has fur on the thick pads of its paws, helping it to grip on the ice.
♦ *The lammergeier drops the bones of its prey onto the rocks below to split them open, so it can feed on the bone marrow.*

LANGURS

Although primarily forest monkeys, langurs (below) also live in many towns and temple grounds. Because Hindus consider them to be sacred animals, they are never harmed and are often fed by people.
♦ *Hindus regard some langurs as the spirit of Hanuman, a kindly monkey king of many legends.*

Rhododendron   Agapetes (a heather relative)

HIMALAYAN FLOWERS

The Himalayas are rich in plant life. There are rare and beautiful orchids, as well as flowering shrubs such as rhododendrons and magnolias. These are now found in gardens around the world.
♦ *The name rhododendron means "rose tree".*

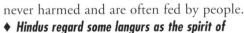

DESERT FESTIVAL

The town of Pushkar, in the Indian state of Rajasthan, holds an annual festival that combines religious worship with a huge livestock fair. The festival has become a popular tourist attraction. Herders come from all over the region to sell their camels and cattle (right). There are camel races, and plenty of singing and dancing. Pushkar has Muslim and Hindu shrines, where pilgrims can worship.

♦ *Camels are ideally suited to Rajasthan's desert conditions because they can go for months without water.*

MANGROVE SWAMP

The delta formed by the Ganges and Brahmaputra rivers in Bangladesh and northeast India contains the biggest mangrove swamp in the world, called the Sundarbans. Mangrove trees grow on flat, muddy ground on tropical coasts. They have adapted to living where salty sea water and fresh river water meet. Some have developed vertical extensions on the roots that are exposed at low tide and allow the plants to breathe. The swamp is home to the rare Sundarbans tiger, which preys on spotted, or chital, deer.

♦ *The mouths of the Ganges and Brahmaputra rivers form the largest delta in the world.*

RAJASTHAN PLAINS

Millions of years ago, Rajasthan (below) was covered in forest. Today, little of it remains except in protected areas such as the Ranthambor National Park, a sanctuary for tigers. Elsewhere the trees have been chopped down to make way for farmland, or to provide people with fuel for heating and cooking. In this dry region of desert and semidesert, drought is often a problem. Irrigation canals have been built so that crops such as millet, sorghum and wheat can be grown. The biggest canal is the Indira Gandhi canal, which brings water from northern rivers.

♦ *Ancient, fossilized tree trunks can be found on the surface of the Thar Desert in Rajasthan.*

Chital deer

Mangrove tree root extensions

THE COBRA AND THE MONGOOSE

Cobras are deadly poisonous snakes that can be up to 5.5 m (18 ft) long. To scare attackers, a cobra rears up and spreads out a hood around its neck. An unlikely enemy is the Indian mongoose, which measures just 25 cm (10 in) long. Fast and alert, it can dodge the snake's fangs and jump in with a killing bite to the neck.

♦ *The Indian mongoose is sometimes kept as a pet to keep people's homes free from rats, mice and snakes.*

Sundarbans tiger

Scarlet ibis

Southern Asia:
Farming and industry

Two out of every three people in Southern Asia make their living from raising crops or keeping animals. Almost everyone in the poorer countries such as Afghanistan, Nepal and Bhutan live off the land. But the cities of India and Pakistan are home to new, growing industries that supply goods to the region's millions of people. They also export textiles, machines and computers to the rest of the world. Throughout Southern Asia, making crafts is an important small industry. Carpets, copperware, leather, jewellery and wooden goods are both sold to tourists and exported. Slowly these activities are raising standards of living.

BOMBAY

Bombay, also called Mumbai, is one of India's great cities. It was originally built on islands in swampland. Because it has the best harbour on the west coast, Portuguese and British traders settled there. It became the commercial and industrial heart of India, with factories making textiles, clothes, bicycles and other goods. A quarter of India's manufactured goods are made in Bombay. Millions of people from the countryside have come to the city. Many cannot find work, however, and they live in flimsy shelters or slums.

♦ *Bombay is the centre of India's large film industry. Indians all over the world can watch films that were made in "Bollywood".*

SPICE MARKET

In the wetter regions of Southern Asia, people eat a lot of rice, while in drier areas, they make flat naan and chapatti bread from wheat or millet. Most meals are simple. Common dishes include dal, a kind of porridge made from lentils and beans, cooked vegetables, and yogurt. Meat is rarely eaten by most people. Following the rules of their religion, Muslims do not eat pork, and Hindus do not eat beef. Dishes are subtly flavored with all kinds of spices and tend to be hotter in the south. Spices include cardamom, turmeric, pepper, clove and cumin. People buy their spices from open-air markets, such as this one in Jaipur, India (right).

♦ *The Arabian Sea coast of the Indian state of Kerala was known to merchants as the Spice Coast because of its wealth of spices.*

STILT FISHING

For the many coastal villages throughout Southern Asia, fishing is an important way of life. Some traditional fishing methods have remained unchanged for centuries. In Kerala in southwest India, fishermen stretch a big net between the beach and a boat, and bands of people help drag the net back to shore. In Sri Lanka, men fish from stilts driven into the sea bed (above). They perch on their stilts and fish with a rod and line. The positions of the stilts are highly valued and are passed on from father to son.

♦ *Fishing is the most important industry in the Maldives, employing a quarter of all workers. There are over a thousand different kinds of local fish.*

SHIPBREAKING

Although Southern Asia has many huge industries, there are also thousands of smaller workshops and factories throughout the region. Many of these enterprises use recycled materials and recondition unwanted goods. Nothing is allowed to go to waste. The shipbuilding industry is an example of recycling on a large scale. At Chittagong in Bangladesh, old ships are broken down into scrap (above left), to supply iron, steel, electrical parts and anything else that can be salvaged. On a smaller scale, people in towns and cities recover glass, metal and paper from rubbish dumps for recycling.

♦ *As well as being the country's main port, Chittagong is a major industrial centre of Bangladesh. It has jute mills, textile factories, engineering works and oil refineries.*

WORKING ELEPHANTS

Many of Southern Asia's forests are in hilly regions that vehicles cannot reach. Foresters often use elephants to shift logs and carry heavy loads. The elephants are trained when young by their handlers, called *mahouts*, to use their trunk and tusks to lift heavy logs. An elephant's trunk is very flexible – it has over 40,000 muscles along its length. Elephants were also once used to carry hunters through the forest and troops into battle.

♦ *Asian elephants are still found in the wild in India's Assam and West Bengal regions, and in Bangladesh.*

FARMING REGIONS

Crops and farming in Southern Asia vary according to climate. Rice fields called paddies are found in areas that receive heavy monsoon rains. In the northern plains of India and Pakistan, where the Indus and Ganges rivers provide irrigation, farmers grow wheat and millet. In the dry lands of Afghanistan and Pakistan, cotton is the main crop. In the mountain regions of the Himalayas, nomads herd yaks, goats and sheep.

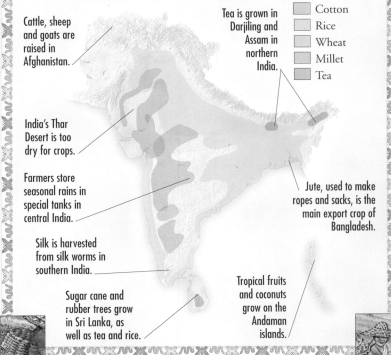

Cattle, sheep and goats are raised in Afghanistan.

Tea is grown in Darjiling and Assam in northern India.

Cotton
Rice
Wheat
Millet
Tea

India's Thar Desert is too dry for crops.

Farmers store seasonal rains in special tanks in central India.

Jute, used to make ropes and sacks, is the main export crop of Bangladesh.

Silk is harvested from silk worms in southern India.

Sugar cane and rubber trees grow in Sri Lanka, as well as tea and rice.

Tropical fruits and coconuts grow on the Andaman islands.

TEA HARVEST

Tea comes from a shrub native to Asia. It grows best in areas of high rainfall and at altitudes of 1,000 to 2,000 m (3,300 to 6,600 ft). India's Assam region, northern Bangladesh and Sri Lanka are some of the world's main tea-growing regions. The buds and smallest leaves are picked from the bushes.

♦ *People have been drinking tea for at least 4,000 years, and it is the world's most popular hot drink.*

MODERN TECHNOLOGY

India is mainly a country of farms and villages, but it also has a rapidly growing industrial economy. Heavy industries such as iron and steel are found in Bihar, West Bengal and Orissa. India's plentiful coal supplies fuel these industries. The country also has advanced hi-tech industries building planes, rockets and satellites. The centre of India's growing computer industry is the city of Bangalore, where these workers (left) are writing software programs. Hundreds of other factories make less expensive goods, such as bicycles and sewing machines.

♦ *In India, many cars are made from designs licensed by foreign companies.*

53

	BRUNEI	CAMBODIA	INDONESIA	LAOS	MALAYSIA	MYANMAR	PALAU	PAPUA NEW GUINEA	PHILIPPINES
Area:	5,765 sq km	181,035 sq km	1,919,443 sq km	236,800 sq km	330,442 sq km	676,577 sq km	458 sq km	462,840 sq km	300,000 sq km
Population:	307,000	10,515,000	203,479,000	5,195,000	21,018,000	46,765,000	15,000	4,500,000	70,724,000

South East Asia

People and places

Tropical South East Asia is made up of thousands of islands and peninsulas. The largest country, Indonesia, has more than 13,000 islands alone. The region's peoples have a long history of trading with each other and with the rest of the world. As a result, the thriving modern cities, such as Djakarta, Singapore and Kuala Lumpur, are a rich mix of cultures, languages and economies. Religious influences include Islamic, Buddhist, Hindu and Christian. In contrast, some remote rural areas have only had contact with the outside world in the past hundred years.

VILLAGE LIFE

Some forest-dwellers in Malaysia and Indonesia still live in the traditional way, in large wooden longhouses. As many as 60 families may live together under one roof. The houses are sometimes more than 200 m (650 ft) long.

◆ The longhouse has a communal veranda and an attic where the villagers store their grain.

ANGKOR WAT

This Hindu temple (left), in the jungle of Cambodia, is part of Angkor Wat, the largest complex of religious buildings in the world. It was built in the 12th century during the Khmer dynasty.

◆ Angkor Wat means "Temple City".

FLOATING MARKET

In much of densely forested South East Asia, waterways are the main link between villages. Thailand is famous for its floating markets. Boats called sampans (right) carry fresh tomatoes, limes, cauliflowers, chillies and other produce along its rivers and Bangkok's canals, which are called klongs.

◆ Thai food includes long-grained rice dishes with vegetables cooked in spices and coconut milk.

STILT HOUSES

In the remote highlands of South East Asia, many people live in villages close to water. This one (right) is in Indonesia. The houses are built on stilts to avoid floods caused by the monsoon rains.

◆ Forest villagers grow crops and collect spices, fruits and other tree produce from the jungle.

54

SINGAPORE
Area: 622 sq km
Population: 3,439,000

THAILAND
Area: 513,115 sq km
Population: 59,159,000

VIETNAM
Area: 331,653 sq km
Population: 76,548,000

SINGAPORE

Singapore, at the tip of the Malay peninsula, is one of the smallest, most prosperous countries in the world. Its wealth comes from its busy port, oil refineries, banking, international trading companies and tourism.

♦ **Modern Singapore was founded in 1819.**

The 7,107 islands of the **Philippines** are of volcanic origin. In 1991 Mount Pinatubo erupted, destroying the homes of 200,000 people.

N

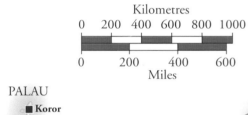

Kilometres

0   200   400   600   800   1000

0   200   400   600
Miles

PETRONAS TOWERS

These twin office towers in Kuala Lumpur, the capital of Malaysia, form the world's tallest building. The Petronas Towers are 452 m (1,483 ft) high, 9 m (30 ft) higher than Chicago's Sears Tower. At the 50th of their 88 floors, the towers are joined by a glass-covered bridge. The Malaysian government built the towers to show the world how advanced their country has become.

♦ **Kuala Lumpur is a modern city where mosques and temples stand alongside freeways and skyscrapers.**

BALINESE DANCER

On the Indonesian island of Bali, a special dance style includes precise movements of the fingers and head.

♦ **Balinese culture is influenced by the Hindu religion.**

PALAU
■ **Koror**

Bougainville

New Britain

P A C I F I C

O C E A N

Jayapura ●

PAPUA
NEW GUINEA
Port Moresby

▲ *Puncak Jaya*

New Guinea

Over 700 different local languages are spoken by the tribes of **Papua New Guinea.**

A N D A

S E A

S   I   A

E

Dili

SHWE DAGON PAGODA

According to legend, the Shwe Dagon Pagoda, a Buddhist temple in Rangoon, Myanmar (right), contains relics of the Buddha himself. It is Myanmar's holiest shrine, and is covered in gold and inlaid with precious stones.

♦ **Shwe Dagon's bell-shaped dome, or stupa, is 99 m (325 ft) high.**

Data file

Area	4,958,750 sq km/1,914,588 sq mi
Population	502 million
Independent countries	12
Largest country	Indonesia (1,919,443 sq km/741,103 sq mi)
Smallest country	Palau (458 sq km/177 sq mi)
Most populated country	Indonesia (203,479,000)
Least populated country	Palau (15,000)
Largest cities	Djakarta, Indonesia (8.3 million); Bangkok, Thailand (5.6 million); Ho Chi Minh City, Vietnam (3.2 million)
Highest mountain	Puncak Jaya, Indonesia (5,039 m/16,502 ft)
Longest river	Mekong, Laos/Cambodia/Vietnam (part) (4,180 km/2,597 mi)
Largest lake	Tonle Sap, Cambodia (10,000 sq km/3,860 sq mi, in the wet season)
Religions	Muslim, Buddhist, Christian, Hindu
Languages	National languages

How places got their names

Bangkok	from the Thai for *village of the wild plum*
Cambodia	from Cambu, the ancestor of the Khmers
Kuala Lumpur	from the Malay for *muddy river mouth*
Philippines	after King Philip II of Spain
Vietnam	from the Vietnamese for *land of the south*

South East Asia:
Nature, farming and industry

South East Asia is rich in natural resources such as timber, oil, gold, tin and rubber. These resources have enabled countries such as Malaysia, Singapore and Indonesia to grow and develop. Other countries, for example Laos and Papua New Guinea, have not yet achieved this development. The region's forests, mangrove swamps and surrounding seas are home to a huge variety of wildlife. Many plants and animals are under threat from logging, dam-building and clearing land for farming.

OIL AND GAS

South East Asia has enough oil and natural gas to supply its own needs and to export abroad. Oil is extracted on land in Sumatra, Malaysia and Borneo, and offshore in the Gulf of Thailand.

♦ *Singapore is a major centre of oil refining.*

Prince Rudolph's blue

Enamelled

White-plumed

Little king

FOREST ANIMALS AND PLANTS

The tropical rainforests of South East Asia are particularly rich in plant and animal species, especially on the islands of Borneo and New Guinea, which have been less disturbed by humans. Strange and unique plants include the giant, parasitic rafflesia, the world's largest flower, and the insect-eating pitcher plants.

♦ *The proboscis monkey, found in Borneo, gets its name from its unusually long nose.*

Green python

Lar gibbon

Proboscis monkey

Tree shrew

BIRDS OF PARADISE

There are 49 species of these amazing, colourful birds (left). Almost all of them are found only on the island of New Guinea. They have evolved fantastic feathers, including fans, plumes and tail streamers up to 60 cm (24 in) long. The birds use these in courtship displays.

♦ *The dramatic display of plumage by male birds of paradise is often accompanied by calls that sound like the crack of a whip.*

MODERN TECHNOLOGY

Modern factories in the region specialize in the manufacture of hi-tech goods. Singapore is a major centre for printing. Skilled workers use the latest technology to produce books, magazines, packaging and other printed products for clients all over the world (above).

♦ *Companies from Japan, Europe and the USA have opened plants and offices across South East Asia.*

Pineapple

Durian

Mango

Banana

Coconut

TROPICAL FRUIT

Many tropical fruits, such as pineapples, coconuts, bananas and mangoes, are grown in the region. Indonesia and the Philippines grow over half the world's coconuts, and Thailand produces a fifth of the world's pineapples. The durian is a large fruit that grows up to 20 cm (8 in) across. It has a hard, thorny husk and cream coloured flesh.

♦ *Durians give off such a powerful smell that some airlines do not allow passengers to carry them aboard their planes.*

IRRIGATED RICE TERRACES

Rice has been the staple crop and traditional food of the region for thousands of years. There are thousands of varieties of rice, each suited to different conditions of climate, soil and altitude. In more populated areas, farmers grow rice in paddy fields or on hillside terraces, such as these on the island of Bali (right). The terraces are irrigated to keep the rice plants under water while they grow. In areas with less rainfall, crops like cassava are grown.

♦ *Plant scientists cross-breed rice plants to produce improved varieties so that farmers can have two or more harvests a year.*

LOGGING

The forests that cover so much of this region contain valuable resources. Hardwood trees such as teak are prized for making expensive furniture. Kapur trees are used for building houses. Trees also supply plywood, paper and resin. After the trees have been felled, they are floated down rivers to mills on the coast, like these logs in Sarawak, Malaysia (above). Many countries have banned the export of logs in order to encourage their own factories to process them into wood and paper. Over-exploitation of the region's forests in countries such as Thailand and the Philippines has caused great damage to the environment.

♦ *In 1997-98, forest fires swept across Borneo, Indonesia, endangering animals such as the orang-utan.*

RUBBER TAPPING

Natural rubber comes from the milky sap of trees that grow in tropical climates such as Phuket island, in Thailand (below). Grooves cut into the bark channel the sap into containers secured to the trunk, where it is collected. This process is called rubber tapping. The sticky substance is rolled into balls for delivery to the factory, where it is made into rubber.

♦ *Malaysia's many large rubber plantations produce half the world's natural rubber.*

Pitcher plant

Rafflesia

MUDSKIPPERS

In the mangrove swamps around the Indian Ocean, strange fish called mudskippers cling to tree roots or lie on the mudflats. They have gills and can breathe under water, but spend most of their time out of water. As long as they remain moist, mudskippers can stay alive by breathing air. They use their pelvic fins like legs to scamper across the muddy surface, feeding off algae, worms and shrimps.

♦ *Mudskippers' eyes can swivel to give them all-round vision.*

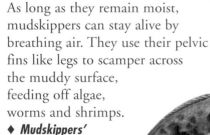

At its lowest, the **Turfan Depression** lies 154 m (505 ft) below sea level.

China
and its neighbours
People and places

China is the world's third largest country and, with over a billion people, is the most populated country on Earth. It has one of the world's oldest civilizations, dating back about 5,000 years. Among the great inventions of the ancient Chinese were the compass, gunpowder and the art of papermaking. Chinese religion, art and architecture have had an important influence on the culture of Taiwan and Korea. In 1949, a Communist government was formed and sweeping changes were made to Chinese society. Today, China is the world's largest Communist country. Korea is divided into a Communist northern state and a democratic southern state.

THE GREAT WALL

The continuous Great Wall of China was started in 221 BC and was built to defend the northern provinces from attack.

♦ **A force of 300,000 slaves built the stone wall.**

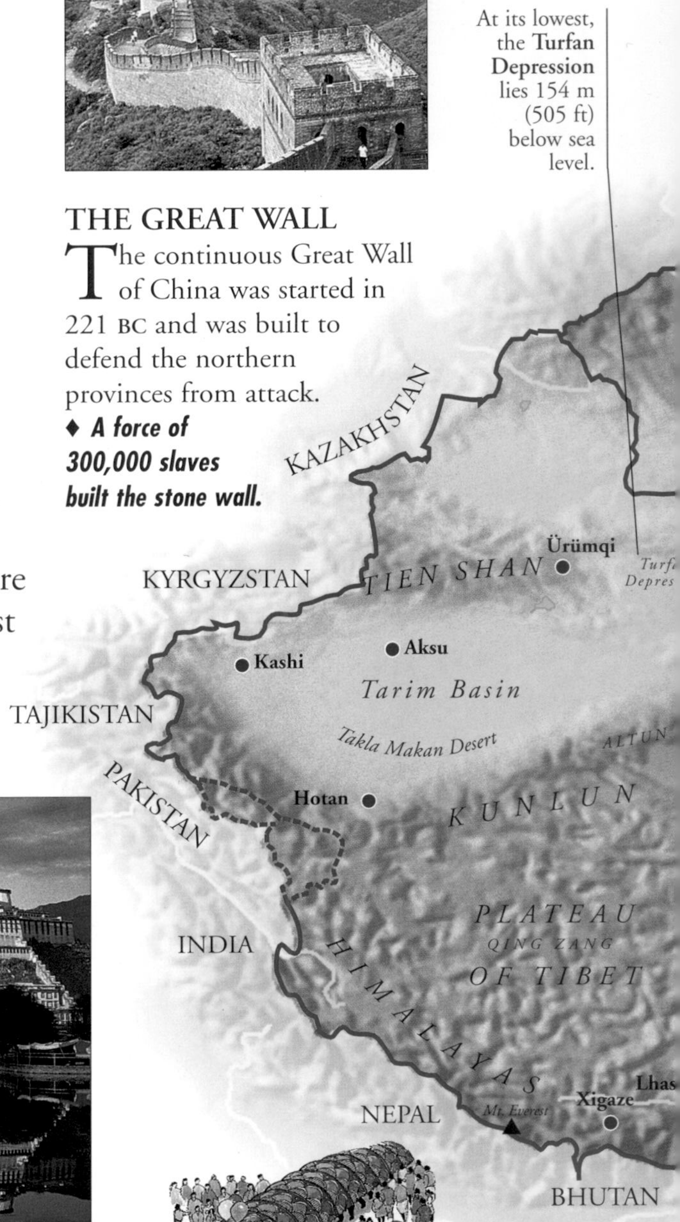

POTALA PALACE

This magnificent palace in Lhasa was built for the Dalai Lama, the spiritual ruler of Tibet. Started in the 17th century, it was added to over the centuries until it had over 1,000 rooms. In 1950, China occupied Tibet and repressed Buddhism, forcing the Dalai Lama to leave in 1959. Today Tibet is a self-governing region of China.

♦ **Lhasa was once called the Forbidden City because visitors were discouraged.**

KAZAKHSTAN

KYRGYZSTAN

TAJIKISTAN

PAKISTAN

INDIA

NEPAL

BHUTAN

TIEN SHAN • Ürümqi   Turfan Depres.

• Kashi   • Aksu

Tarim Basin

Takla Makan Desert

Hotan •   KUNLUN   ALTUN

PLATEAU QING ZANG OF TIBET

HIMALAYAS

Mt. Everest ▲   Xigaze •   Lhas...

TERRACOTTA ARMY

In 1974 workers digging a well near Xi'an in China discovered 7,500 life-sized model soldiers made from terracotta. They were found in the tomb of the emperor Qin Shih Huang Ti (259–210 BC), first emperor of the whole of China.

♦ **Xi'an was the ancient capital of the Han Chinese.**

DRAGON DANCE

To celebrate the Chinese New Year, people make huge paper dragons and carry them through the streets. Firecrackers are let off to frighten away evil spirits. The Chinese New Year marks the start of spring and its date varies according to the phases of the moon. It can take place between 21 January and 20 February.

♦ **New Year is the Chinese people's most important holiday. Families get together to exchange gifts.**

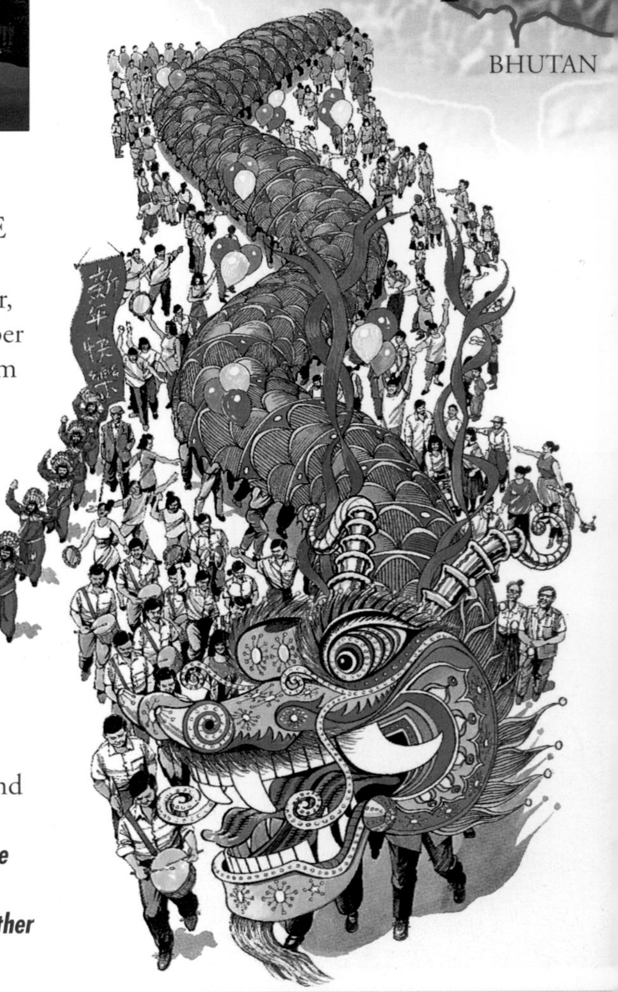

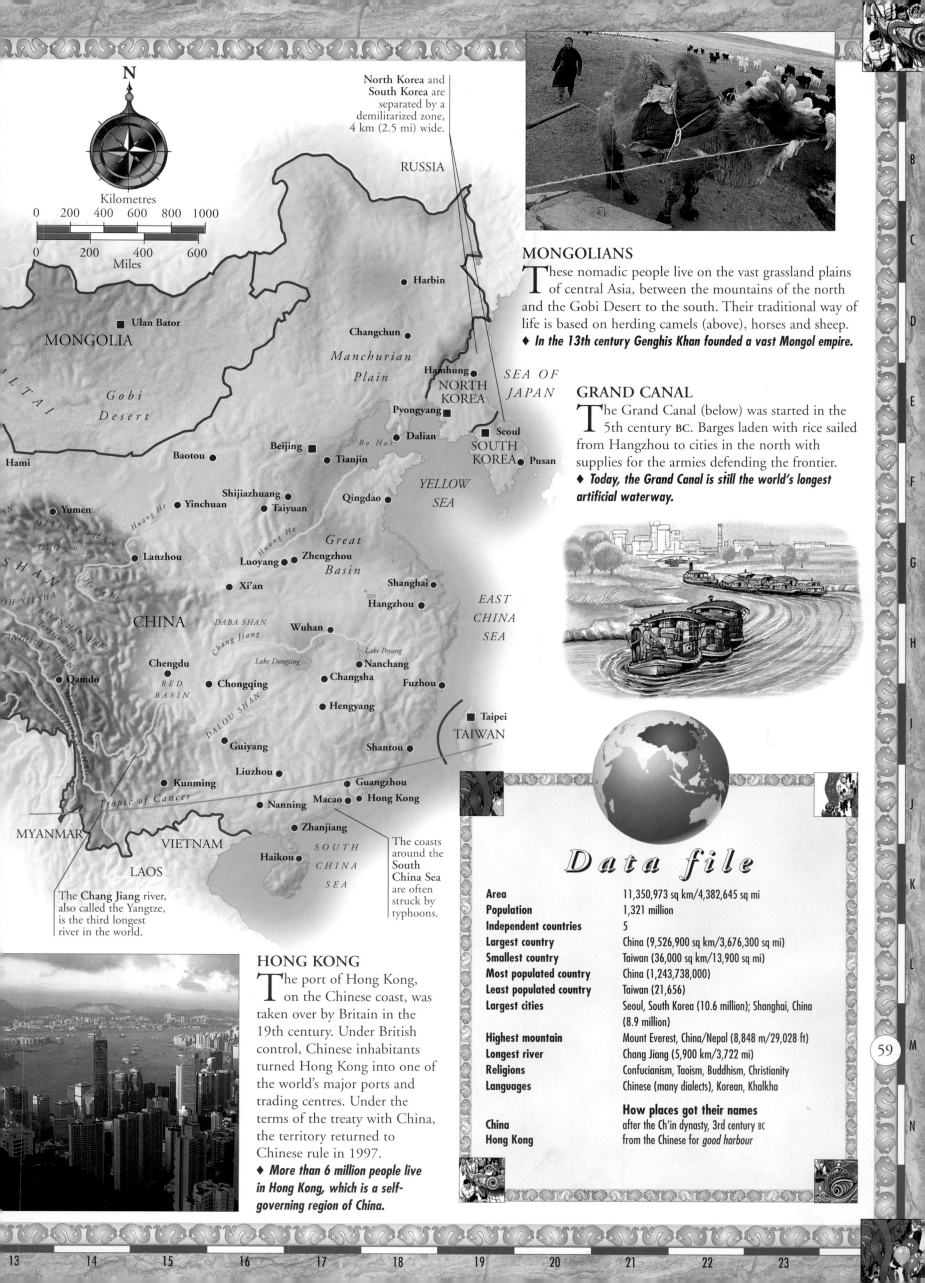

North Korea and South Korea are separated by a demilitarized zone, 4 km (2.5 mi) wide.

RUSSIA

Harbin

Changchun

Manchurian Plain

Ulan Bator

MONGOLIA

Gobi Desert

Hamhung

NORTH KOREA

SEA OF JAPAN

Pyongyang

Dalian

Seoul

SOUTH KOREA

Pusan

Hami

Beijing

Baotou

Tianjin

Bo Hai

Yumen

Shijiazhuang

Yinchuan

Taiyuan

Qingdao

YELLOW SEA

QILIAN SHAN

Lanzhou

Luoyang

Zhengzhou

Great Basin

Shanghai

SHAN

Xi'an

Hangzhou

EAST CHINA SEA

OH XILSHA

CHINA

DABA SHAN

Wuhan

BAYAN HAR SHAN

Chang Jiang

Lake Dongting

Lake Poyang

Nanchang

Chengdu

RED BASIN

Chongqing

Changsha

Fuzhou

Qamdo

Hengyang

DALOU SHAN

Taipei

TAIWAN

Guiyang

Shantou

Liuzhou

Kunming

Guangzhou

MYANMAR

Nanning

Macao

Hong Kong

Tropic of Cancer

Zhanjiang

VIETNAM

Haikou

SOUTH CHINA SEA

The coasts around the **South China Sea** are often struck by typhoons.

LAOS

The **Chang Jiang** river, also called the Yangtze, is the third longest river in the world.

Kilometres
0 200 400 600 800 1000
0 200 400 600
Miles

MONGOLIANS

These nomadic people live on the vast grassland plains of central Asia, between the mountains of the north and the Gobi Desert to the south. Their traditional way of life is based on herding camels (above), horses and sheep.
♦ *In the 13th century Genghis Khan founded a vast Mongol empire.*

GRAND CANAL

The Grand Canal (below) was started in the 5th century BC. Barges laden with rice sailed from Hangzhou to cities in the north with supplies for the armies defending the frontier.
♦ *Today, the Grand Canal is still the world's longest artificial waterway.*

HONG KONG

The port of Hong Kong, on the Chinese coast, was taken over by Britain in the 19th century. Under British control, Chinese inhabitants turned Hong Kong into one of the world's major ports and trading centres. Under the terms of the treaty with China, the territory returned to Chinese rule in 1997.
♦ *More than 6 million people live in Hong Kong, which is a self-governing region of China.*

Data file

Area	11,350,973 sq km/4,382,645 sq mi
Population	1,321 million
Independent countries	5
Largest country	China (9,526,900 sq km/3,676,300 sq mi)
Smallest country	Taiwan (36,000 sq km/13,900 sq mi)
Most populated country	China (1,243,738,000)
Least populated country	Taiwan (21,656)
Largest cities	Seoul, South Korea (10.6 million); Shanghai, China (8.9 million)
Highest mountain	Mount Everest, China/Nepal (8,848 m/29,028 ft)
Longest river	Chang Jiang (5,900 km/3,722 mi)
Religions	Confucianism, Taoism, Buddhism, Christianity
Languages	Chinese (many dialects), Korean, Khalkha
	How places got their names
China	after the Ch'in dynasty, 3rd century BC
Hong Kong	from the Chinese for *good harbour*

China and its neighbours:
Nature, farming and industry

China's vast population lives mainly in the eastern third of the country. The other two-thirds, and Mongolia, contain some of the world's most remote and inhospitable places. They include the Gobi and Takla Makan deserts, and the high, cold Tibetan plateau. Most of the region's people are farmers. In remote areas the traditional lifestyle is based on herding. China has vast mineral wealth, and large reserves of coal and petroleum. Factories in Taiwan, South Korea and the Guangdong area of China make many of the toys, shoes, mobile phones and other goods used by people all over the world.

STEAM LOCOMOTIVES

To carry heavy freight such as coal, as well as passengers, across China, the country has over 58,000 km (36,000 mi) of railway. Over half of China's trains are still pulled by steam locomotives, such as this one (above) in Changchun. Most of the track is found in the crowded eastern regions, and only since the 1970s have new lines been laid to the remoter regions of the north and west.
♦ *Many of the more isolated Chinese settlements rely today on air travel.*

TAKLA MAKAN DESERT

The desert summers are very hot and the winters very cold. Rivers that run down from the mountains often dry up. Yet many hoofed animals, such as asses, gazelles and antelopes, live in the desert. Herds of wild asses, though now less common than they once were, roam huge distances as they search for grass.
♦ *The wild ass, or onager, is a fast runner and can go for two or three days without drinking.*

Gazelle

Wild ass

Argali

LIMESTONE HILLS

The hills of Guilin in southern China are famous natural wonders. They rise almost vertically from the rice fields around them, and have been a popular subject of Chinese paintings since ancient times. The hills are made of limestone, which is easily worn away by rainwater. Over millions of years this has left steep hills, like towers, with many caves inside.
♦ *The fertile south produces two crops of rice a year, and a third crop of vegetables.*

FISHING WITH CORMORANTS

On the river Li in southern China fishermen use cormorants to catch fish. The birds dive under water to make their catch, but a ring around their throats prevents them from swallowing the fish. Fishermen usually go out at night and use lanterns to attract the fish.
♦ *Many Chinese villages have special ponds that are used for fish farming.*

SHIPYARDS

South Korea and Taiwan are two of the world's leaders in shipbuilding. Only Japan builds more ships. This vessel (right) is in a dry dock at Kaohsiung, a deepwater port in Taiwan. After entering the dock, the ship was placed on supports and the water drained out. Dry docks allow repairs to be made. Shipbreakers take old vessels apart and then recycle metal and other materials. For a small country like Taiwan, which has few natural resources of its own, this is a useful way to provide iron and steel. It helps Taiwan compete with countries that can make ships with their own resources.
♦ *South Korea's official name is the Republic of Korea; North Korea is the Democratic People's Republic of Korea.*

CHINESE FOOD

In the south of China people mostly eat rice, but in the north they eat noodles, steamed buns and bread made from wheat. The staple foods are served with a great variety of spicy sauces. This Kaili woman from Guizo (right) is hanging out noodles to dry.

♦ *Milk is taken from cattle, sheep, goats and water buffalo.*

Red panda

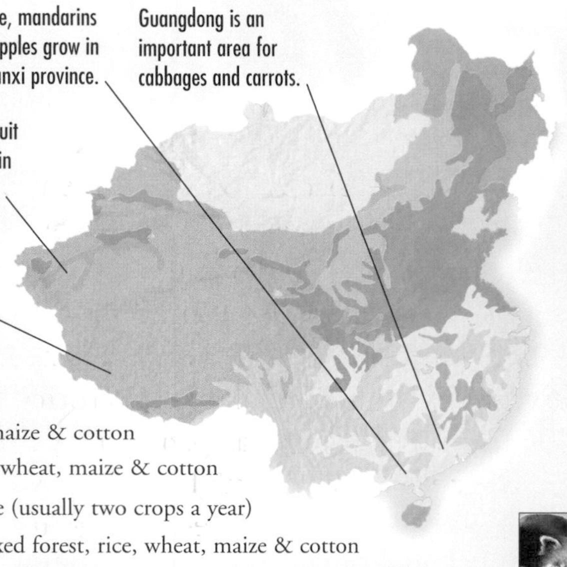

ELECTRONICS

South Korea and Taiwan have built up their economies by specializing in making goods for export. They began with low-cost goods such as pocket calculators and digital watches. Later, they developed advanced computer industries (below).

♦ *Many workers in the electronics factories of the Far East are women.*

CHINA'S FARMING REGIONS

Only one-tenth of China's land area is suitable for cultivation. Half of this is given over to paddy fields or irrigated for other crops such as cabbages and carrots. Rice, the main crop, is grown mainly in the south. Almost one-third of China is used for herding livestock, raised mainly for meat.

Sugar cane, mandarins and pineapples grow in warm Guanxi province.

Guangdong is an important area for cabbages and carrots.

Melons and other fruit are grown in oases in the western deserts.

Yaks are raised on the high plateau of Tibet.

- Forest
- Herding
- Wheat, maize & cotton
- Herding, wheat, maize & cotton
- Rice (usually two crops a year)
- Mixed forest, rice, wheat, maize & cotton

BAMBOO FOREST

The mountains of central China were once covered in huge areas of bamboo forest. Over the centuries so much forest has been cut down that animals such as the giant panda have become rare. Bamboo leaves and shoots are not very nutritious, so giant pandas spend two-thirds of their time eating.

♦ *Bamboo is actually a type of grass. It is the fastest-growing plant in the world.*

Golden pheasant

Musk deer

Bamboo

Giant panda

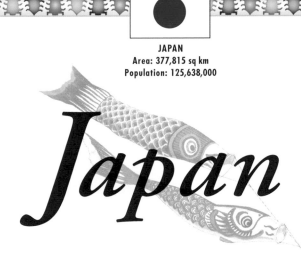

JAPAN
Area: 377,815 sq km
Population: 125,638,000

Japan

Japan consists of four large islands and four thousand smaller ones lying between the northern Pacific Ocean and the mainland of Asia. It is a land of violent natural forces, with frequent earthquakes, over a hundred volcanoes and fierce storms called typhoons. But it also has great natural beauty in its mountains, forests and famous gardens of cherry trees. Japan is a fascinating mixture of ancient and modern. There are thousands of Buddhist and Shinto shrines where religious festivals are held. After the devastation of World War II, Japan rebuilt itself to become one of the world's major industrial powers.

TOKYO, JAPAN'S CAPITAL

Tokyo city is part of the largest built-up area in the world. Over 30 million people live in the city and its suburbs. It is so big that people have to travel long distances in fast, packed commuter trains to get to work. Tokyo is famous for its giant department stores. The Ginza (above) is a popular shopping district.
♦ *Many of the world's leading companies are based in Tokyo. It is also an important banking centre.*

JAPANESE FOOD

A typical Japanese meal consists of rice, soup called miso, made from soya beans, and a number of small side dishes called kazu (right). Other favourite foods include raw fish, either on its own (called sashimi) or with rice (sushi). Japanese chefs present dishes with great skill and artistic feeling.
♦ *Fugu, or blowfish, is a great delicacy. It is so poisonous that it has to be cooked by specially trained chefs.*

RICE FARMING

So much of Japan is covered in mountains, forests or areas of poor soil that there is very little farmland to feed the large population. Japanese farmers have learned how to make the most of small plots of land to grow enough rice for the country. They have invented new strains of rice that produce more food, and they use pesticides, fertilizers and automated rice harvesters (above).
♦ *Most rice farmers work part-time in factories and offices.*

WORKING ROBOTS

Although Japan has few natural resources, it is one of the world's most successful manufacturing countries. Japanese car factories use specially designed robots for many tasks, such as welding (below) in Nissan's factory near Tokyo.
♦ *Japan's factories make more cars and cameras than any other country.*

The city of **Hiroshima** was where the first atomic bomb was dropped by the USA on August 6th, 1945.

The Inland Sea is 418 km (260 mi) long and up to 70 km (43 mi) wide.

Kyushu is a volcanic island with many hot springs.

SEA OF JAPAN

Suzu-misaki

Kanazawa • Toya

▲ Haku-san

Fukui •

Dogo

Dozen

OKI-SHOTO

Matsue •

Kyoto • Nagoya • Toyota

Okayama • Kobe • Toyohashi

Harima-nada

J A P A N

Osaka • Hamamat

Hiroshima •

Kure • Takamatsu

Tsushima

Matsuyama • Tokushima

Shimonoseki

Kita-kyushu • Suo-nada

Shikoku

Wakayama

• Fukuoka

• Kochi

• Sasebo

Bungo Channel

• Omuta

Nagasaki • • Kumamoto

Kyushu

Sendai

• Miyazaki

N

• Kagoshima

Kilometres
0   50   100   150   200 250 300 350

0   50   100   150   200
Miles

The **Seikan Tunnel** linking Hokkaido and Honshu islands is the world's longest undersea tunnel (54 km/34 mi long).

Honshu is the world's seventh largest island (227,415 sq km/87,806 sq mi).

KOBE EARTHQUAKE

Japan is located where three of the giant plates which make up the Earth's crust meet. When these plates move against each other, earthquakes occur. There are over 1,500 in Japan each year. In 1995 a severe earthquake destroyed the city of Kobe (right), killing 5,000 people.

♦ The scientists who study and try to predict earthquakes are called seismologists.

OFFSHORE AIRPORT

There is so little flat land in Japan that planners have to find new ways to make room for building. In Osaka Bay they have built a whole airport on a man-made island 5 km (3 mi) from the coast. Aircraft land and take off over the sea, which means that Kansai airport (below) can operate 24 hours a day without the noise disturbing anyone.

♦ Tokyo's business districts have been extended onto land reclaimed from the sea in Tokyo Bay.

JAPANESE CHILDREN

These children (above right) are visiting the famous Yomeimon Gate at Toshoga shrine in Nikko. Japanese families are usually small and children are greatly valued by their parents. They receive lots of toys, and often have their own television and telephone. Children are expected to work very hard at school. Many attend special classes to help them do better in exams and win a place at a top university.

♦ In Japan, May 5th is a national holiday called Children's Day.

MACAQUES

Japanese macaques are found further north than any other monkey. They live in troops of up to 100 monkeys. They usually spend the day in trees eating leaves, but they are also good swimmers. In winter, they keep warm by bathing in hot springs (left). Macaques are very quick to learn new ways. One troop on Koshima Island taught each other how to wash their sweet potatoes before eating them.

♦ Japanese macaques store their food in cheek pouches.

Data file

Area	377,815 sq km/145,875 sq mi
Population	126 million
Capital city	Tokyo
Largest cities	Tokyo (city 11.9 million), Yokohama (3.3 million), Osaka (2.5 million)
Highest mountain	Mount Fuji (3,776 m/12,388 ft)
Longest river	Shinano (368 km/229 mi)
Largest lake	Biwa (674 sq km/260 sq mi)
Religions	Shintoism, Buddhism
Currency	1 yen = 100 sen

How places got their names

Hokkaido	from the Japanese for *northern land*
Honshu	from the Japanese for *chief island*
Tokyo	from the Japanese for *eastern capital*

ALGERIA
Area: 2,381,741 sq km
Population: 29,473,000

ANGOLA
Area: 1,246,700 sq km
Population: 11,570,000

BENIN
Area: 112,600 sq km
Population: 5,720,000

BOTSWANA
Area: 581,730 sq km
Population: 1,518,000

BURKINA FASO
Area: 274,200 sq km
Population: 11,087,000

BURUNDI
Area: 25,967 sq km
Population: 6,398,000

CAMEROON
Area: 463,511 sq km
Population: 13,937,000

CAPE VERDE
Area: 4,033 sq km
Population: 406,000

CENTRAL AFRICAN REPUBLIC
Area: 622,436 sq km
Population: 3,416,000

Africa
People and places

Straddling the Equator, the huge, hot continent of Africa makes up a fifth of the world's land area and is the second largest continent. It is the home of hundreds of native peoples with their own cultures, beliefs and languages; there are more than 250 peoples in Nigeria alone. In north Africa, Arabic is the common language and Islam is the main religion. West Africa — colonized in the 19th century mainly by the French, British and Portuguese — is dominated by farming and logging. South Africa, with its vast mineral deposits, is the wealthiest of the southern countries. In many of the 53 countries, civil wars and unstable governments cause the people great hardship.

The **Sahara Desert** is the world's largest desert. Temperatures can be hotter than 50° C (120° F).

Statue of Liberty 91.5 m (300 ft)

Great Pyramid 147m (482 ft)

Sydney Opera House 67.4 m (221 ft)

Lake Volta, at 8,482 sq km (3,275 sq mi), is the world's largest artificial lake.

THE GREAT RIFT VALLEY

A series of valleys, called the Great Rift Valley, extends for 6,000 km (3,750 mi) all the way from the Red Sea to Mozambique. It was made millions of years ago when the land slipped down between huge cracks, called faults, in the Earth's crust.
♦ *Parts of the Great Rift Valley have become deep lakes, such as Lake Nyasa in Malawi.*

MASAI PEOPLE

The Masai are cattle herders. They live on the grasslands of Kenya and Tanzania. Men may have several wives. Women and girls shave their heads and wear elaborate bead neckbands.
♦ *The Masai diet includes milk, blood and meat.*

LIFE IN THE VILLAGE

Many Africans live in traditional village homes built from earth, wood, grass and sometimes animal skins. Other dwellings are built from bricks and have thatched roofs, such as these in Zimbabwe (above). Village huts are sometimes grouped together inside a fence or stockade, which also holds cattle, goats and chickens.
♦ *The head of the family usually has his own room. Children sleep with their mother in a separate room.*

The **Cape of Good Hope** is often swept by terrible storms.

Kilometres
0 200 400 600 800 1000

Miles
0 200 400 600

Map labels:
SPAIN, MADEIRA (PORT.), Strait of Gibraltar, Oran, Algiers, Annaba, Casablanca, Rabat, Tunis, MOROCCO, ATLAS MOUNTAINS, TUNISIA, Tripoli, Misratah, Benghazi, CANARY ISLANDS (SPAIN), ALGERIA, Ghadâmes, LIBYA, El Aaiun, In Salah, SAHARA, Marzuq, Libyan Desert, WESTERN SAHARA, F'Dérik, DESERT, AHAGGAR, Mt. Tahat, TIBESTI, MAURITANIA, MALI, Timbuktu, NIGER, CHAD, Lake Chad, Nouakchott, Senegal, Niger, N'Djamena, SENEGAL, Bamako, Ouagadougou, Niamey, Chari, Dakar, GAMBIA, Banjul, BURKINA FASO, NIGERIA, Bissau, GUINEA BISSAU, GUINEA, BENIN, Abuja, CENTRAL AFRICAN REPUBLIC, Conakry, IVORY COAST, GHANA, TOGO, Ibadan, Freetown, SIERRA LEONE, Lake Volta, Lomé, Lagos, Benue, Monrovia, Yamoussoukro, Accra, Porto Novo, CAMEROON, Bangui, LIBERIA, Abidjan, Gulf of Guinea, Malabo, Yaoundé, ATLANTIC OCEAN, EQUATORIAL GUINEA, São Tomé, Libreville, Congo, Kisanga, SAO TOME & PRINCIPE, GABON, DEMOCRATIC REPUBLIC OF CONGO, CONGO, Brazzaville, Kinshasa, Kana, Luanda, ANGOLA PLATEAU, Lobito, ANGOLA, Huambo, ZAMB, Livingsto, NAMIBIA, Okavango Delta, Windhoek, BOTSWAN, Gabor, Kalahari Desert, Tropic of Capricorn, Johannes, SOUTH AFRICA, LESOT, GREAT KAROO, Cape Town, Cape of Good Hope, Namib Desert, Orange

N

CHAD Area: 1,284,000 sq km Population: 6,702,000

COMOROS Area: 1,862 sq km Population: 652,000

CONGO Area: 342,000 sq km Population: 2,743,000

DEMOCRATIC REPUBLIC OF CONGO Area: 2,345,095 sq km Population: 48,040,000

DJIBOUTI Area: 23,200 sq km Population: 634,000

EGYPT Area: 997,739 sq km Population: 64,466,000

EQUATORIAL GUINEA Area: 28,051 sq km Population: 420,000

ERITREA Area: 121,320 sq km Population: 3,409,000

ETHIOPIA Area: 1,119,683 sq km Population: 60,148,000

EGYPT'S PYRAMIDS

Pyramids are enormous, four-sided tombs that were built to hold the mummified bodies of Egyptian kings. The biggest is the Great Pyramid at Giza, which was built about 2500 BC.

♦ **The Great Pyramid is made from more than 2 million blocks of limestone.**

The **Suez Canal** is a vital waterway for ships travelling from Europe to Asia. It connects the Mediterranean Sea to the Red Sea.

At 6,670 km (4,125 mi), the river **Nile** is the world's longest river.

AFRICAN MUSIC

Music plays an important part in the lives of the African peoples. The extraordinary rhythms and exuberant sounds of traditional African music are often produced on drums and stringed instruments — like this one from Gambia in west Africa (below) — made from gourds, animal skins and horns.

♦ **Gambia is Africa's smallest mainland country.**

AFRICA'S LARGEST CITY

Cairo (above) is Egypt's capital and Africa's largest city. Like many African cities, it is bustling and filled with traffic. The minarets of over 400 mosques rise above the packed bazaars of the old quarter and the modern office blocks, banks and hotels of the modern city.

♦ **Cairo's population includes people from many different backgrounds, such as Muslims, Christians, Arabs, Turks, Jews, black Africans and Europeans.**

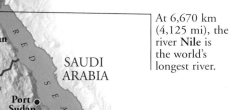

NOMADIC WAY OF LIFE

The Tuaregs are a nomadic people who roam the Sahara Desert with their animals searching for water and fresh pastures. Most nomads ride camels, although trucks are increasingly used today.

♦ **About half a million people live a nomadic life in and around the Sahara Desert.**

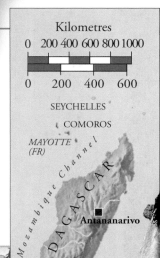

Kilometres

0 200 400 600 800 1000

0   200   400   600

SEYCHELLES
COMOROS
MAYOTTE (FR)

Data file

Area	29,817,713 sq km/11,512,708 sq mi
Population	719 million
Independent countries	53, and 3 dependencies
Largest country	Sudan (2,503,890 sq km/966,757 sq mi)
Smallest country	Seychelles (453 sq km/175 sq mi)
Most populated country	Nigeria (118,369,000)
Least populated country	Seychelles (74,000)
Largest cities	Cairo, Egypt (6.7 million); Lagos, Nigeria (5.7 million)
Highest mountain	Kilimanjaro, Tanzania (5,895 m/19,340 ft)
Longest river	Nile (6,670 km/4,125 mi)
Largest lake	Victoria (69,500 sq km/26,834 sq mi)
Religions	Christian, Dutch Reformed, Ethiopian Orthodox, Hindu, Muslim, local religions
Languages	Hundreds of native languages

How places got their names

Benin, Ghana, Mali	from early African empires
Chad	from Lake Chad
Gambia, Niger, Nigeria	from African rivers
Ivory Coast	from ivory, which was traded there
Namibia	from the Namib Desert
Sierra Leone	from the Portuguese for *lion mountain*
Tanzania	from the first letters of *Tanganyika* and *Zanzibar*, two former independent countries that joined to become Tanzania

65

	GABON		GAMBIA		GHANA		GUINEA		GUINEA-BISSAU		IVORY COAST		KENYA		LESOTHO		LIBERIA
	Area: 267,667 sq km Population: 1,138,000		Area: 10,689 sq km Population: 1,168,000		Area: 238,533 sq km Population: 18,338,000		Area: 245,857 sq km Population: 7,614,000		Area: 36,125 sq km Population: 1,112,000		Area: 320,763 sq km Population: 14,299,000		Area: 571,416 sq km Population: 28,414,000		Area: 30,355 sq km Population: 2,131,000		Area: 99,067 sq km Population: 2,468,000

Africa: *Nature*

Vast areas of unspoilt wilderness can be found all across Africa, from the huge Sahara Desert in the north to the Kalahari and Namib deserts in the far south. Dense tropical rainforest in western and central Africa supports gorillas, giant forest pigs, monkeys and countless birds. Coral reefs flourish in the warm waters off the east coast. Vast stretches of savannah grassland are home to giraffes, rhinos and lions. Africa also has snowcapped volcanic mountains, big rivers, and lakes where pink flamingoes breed. The world's fastest land animal, the cheetah, and the world's largest land animal, the African elephant, are both found on this amazing continent.

DESERT PLANTS

Many African plants are strikingly adapted to drought. Watermelons store water in their stems, while the welwitschia plant of the Namib Desert has a massive taproot that draws on moisture deep beneath the desert's surface.

♦ **The welwitschia may live for as long as 2,000 years.**

Watermelon

Welwitschia

MIGRATION

Millions of wildebeest (above) live on the plains of northern Tanzania and southern Kenya. The seasonal rains fall at different times of year within this region. Vast herds of wildebeest follow the rains to find the best grazing. On their journey, they cross from Tanzania's Serengeti National Park into Kenya by swimming across the Mara river.

♦ **More than 2 million wildebeest cross the Mara river each year between July and October.**

African elephant and calf

Thomson's gazelle

Leopard

LIBYA Area: 1,757,000 sq km Population: 5,784,000
MADAGASCAR Area: 587,041 sq km Population: 15,846,000
MALAWI Area: 94,276 sq km Population: 10,087,000
MALI Area: 1,240,192 sq km Population: 11,480,000
MAURITANIA Area: 1,030,700 sq km Population: 2,392,000
MAURITIUS Area: 2,040 sq km Population: 1,141,000
MOROCCO Area: 458,730 sq km Population: 27,518,000
MOZAMBIQUE Area: 799,379 sq km Population: 18,265,000
NAMIBIA Area: 823,144 sq km Population: 1,613,000

BAOBAB TREE

The tropical African baobab tree (right) has a wide trunk in which it stores water. The swollen trunk helps it survive the dry season.

♦ *The baobab is also called a bottle tree.*

SAVANNAH

Snowcapped Mount Kilimanjaro, in Tanzania, rises above a vast expanse of savannah grassland that stretches as far as the eye can see. The mix of grasses and acacia trees on the savannah supports vast herds of grazing mammals, such as elephants, giraffes, buffaloes, zebras and Thomson's gazelles. These grazers are hunted by predators such as cheetahs, leopards and lions, and they in turn are followed by scavenging hyenas and jackals.

♦ *The giraffe is the tallest animal in the world. It can grow up to 6 m (20 ft) tall.*

Zebra Buffalo Giraffe

PROTECTED AREAS

Throughout Africa there are national parks and reserves that protect important habitats and wildlife from the spread of human beings. These parks also stop people hunting the animals. The most important role of these protected areas is to keep whole environments intact and safe.

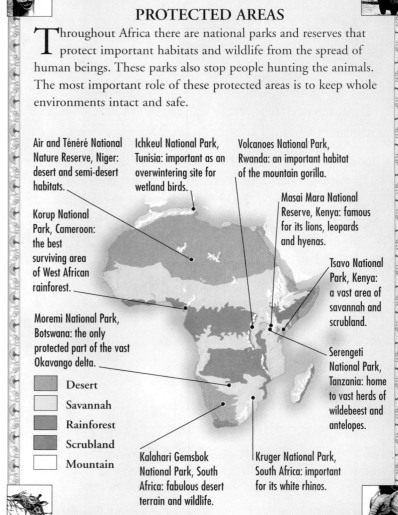

Air and Ténéré National Nature Reserve, Niger: desert and semi-desert habitats.

Ichkeul National Park, Tunisia: important as an overwintering site for wetland birds.

Volcanoes National Park, Rwanda: an important habitat of the mountain gorilla.

Korup National Park, Cameroon: the best surviving area of West African rainforest.

Masai Mara National Reserve, Kenya: famous for its lions, leopards and hyenas.

Tsavo National Park, Kenya: a vast area of savannah and scrubland.

Moremi National Park, Botswana: the only protected part of the vast Okavango delta.

Serengeti National Park, Tanzania: home to vast herds of wildebeest and antelopes.

- Desert
- Savannah
- Rainforest
- Scrubland
- Mountain

Kalahari Gemsbok National Park, South Africa: fabulous desert terrain and wildlife.

Kruger National Park, South Africa: important for its white rhinos.

LIFE IN THE DESERTS

Lack of water is the main problem faced by desert animals. In some areas rain may not fall for years at a time. Many desert animals, such as camels, can go without water for very long periods. Others, like desert vipers and lizards, burrow to escape the intense heat of the sun, and come out at night to search for food. Fennec foxes keep cool by losing heat through their large ears.

♦ *Ostriches live in semidesert areas of the Sahara, Kalahari and Namib deserts.*

Fennec fox Arabian camel Ostrich Lizard Desert viper

RIVERS AND LAKES

Africa has many mighty rivers, such as the Nile, the Congo and the Zambezi. There are spectacular waterfalls, too, like the Victoria Falls, and many shimmering lakes, which are breeding grounds for flamingoes. Many of Africa's rivers and lakes provide a year-round supply of water for the animals that come to drink from them each day. Others are seasonal and last only for a few weeks each year. Hippos and crocodiles (left) are both river creatures, spending most of their time in the water. Hippos emerge onto land only after sunset to graze, and female crocodiles come out to lay their eggs in hollows on the riverbanks.

♦ *The female Nile crocodile may lay as many as 80 eggs in one batch.*

NIGER
Area: 1,186,408 sq km
Population: 9,787,000

NIGERIA
Area: 923,768 sq km
Population: 118,369,000

RWANDA
Area: 26,338 sq km
Population: 5,883,000

SAO TOME
AND PRINCIPE
Area: 1,001 sq km
Population: 117,000

SENEGAL
Area: 196,722 sq km
Population: 8,762,000

SEYCHELLES
Area: 453 sq km
Population: 74,000

SIERRA
LEONE
Area: 71,740 sq km
Population: 4,428,000

SOMALIA
Area: 637,657 sq km
Population: 10,217,000

SOUTH
AFRICA
Area: 1,225,815 sq km
Population: 43,347,000

Africa:
Farming and industry

Africa has a great wealth of mineral and other resources. South Africa, Algeria, Namibia, Zambia and the Democratic Republic of Congo are major suppliers of copper, gold, diamonds, uranium, oil and natural gas to the rest of the world. Mining for these resources, especially in southern Africa, is the most important industry. Many countries in west Africa, as well as Egypt and Kenya, earn money by exporting dates, cotton, tea, coffee, peanuts and palm oil. For many Africans, farming to feed themselves remains the main economic activity. They mostly use traditional tools and methods to grow crops and herd livestock.

TRADITIONAL FARMING

Most African families practise "subsistence" farming using traditional methods (above). They grow enough food for their families, and there may be a little left for sale at market.
♦ **Staple crops include maize, millet, rice, sorghum, bananas, cassava and sweet potatoes.**

VINEYARDS

The dry, warm summers and mild winters of South Africa's climate are ideal for growing grapes, which are used to make wine. Grapevines (above) were first planted in South Africa by Dutch settlers in the mid-1700s. Today there are over 1,000 sq km (386 sq mi) of vineyards stretching inland from Cape Town.
♦ **South Africa's commercial farmers grow sugar cane, citrus fruits and cotton, as well as grapes, for export.**

MARKET DAY

Colourful market scenes, such as this one in Sudan (right), are common throughout Africa. They are an important meeting place; people come from far and wide to sell any surplus vegetables and fruit they have grown, and to exchange news. In many countries the market produce is grown and sold by the women, who also make handmade items such as decorated earthenware pots, hand-printed fabrics and colourful clothes to sell.
♦ **The island of Zanzibar off the coast of Tanzania produces most of the world's cloves, a strong spice used in cooking all over the world.**

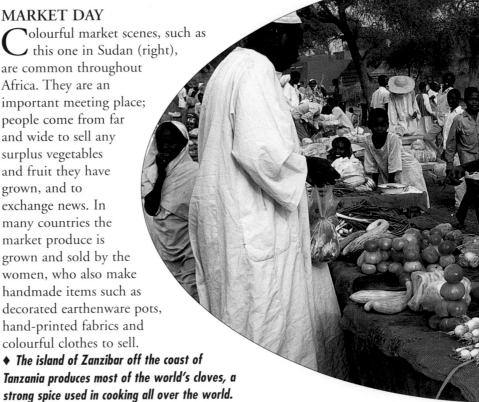

HERDING LIVESTOCK

Today, people from many different African nations herd cattle, goats, sheep and camels in the same way as their ancestors did before them. They allow their livestock to graze on any available grassland, and often travel long distances with their animals looking for new grazing land as the dry and rainy seasons change over. This young Masai herder is leading his cattle to new pastures in Kenya.
♦ **In arid areas of Africa, women and children often have to walk at least 8 km (5 mi) to collect water.**

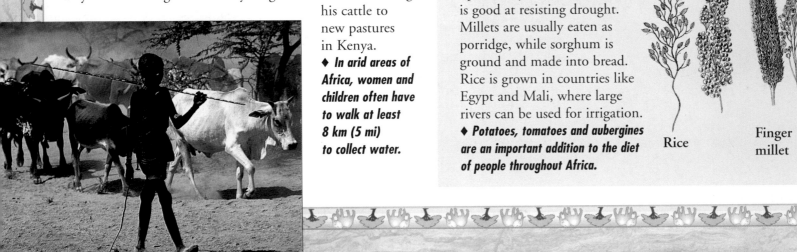

GRAIN CROPS

Millets are grown widely throughout central Africa. Finger millet is rich in minerals and can be stored for up to five years. Bulrush millet is good at resisting drought. Millets are usually eaten as porridge, while sorghum is ground and made into bread. Rice is grown in countries like Egypt and Mali, where large rivers can be used for irrigation.
♦ **Potatoes, tomatoes and aubergines are an important addition to the diet of people throughout Africa.**

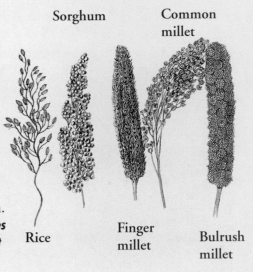

Sorghum

Common millet

Rice

Finger millet

Bulrush millet

SUDAN — Area: 2,503,890 sq km, Population: 27,898,000
SWAZILAND — Area: 17,364 sq km, Population: 906,000
TANZANIA — Area: 885,987 sq km, Population: 31,506,000
TOGO — Area: 56,785 sq km, Population: 4,316,000
TUNISIA — Area: 154,530 sq km, Population: 9,325,000
UGANDA — Area: 197,040 sq km, Population: 20,791,000
ZAMBIA — Area: 752,614 sq km, Population: 8,478,000
ZIMBABWE — Area: 390,759 sq km, Population: 11,682,000

HANDICRAFTS

Colourful handicrafts are made throughout Africa. They are sold for local use as well as to tourists, often directly from the workshops. Morocco is famous for its boldly patterned, hand-knotted carpets and rugs (left). They are hung up for display in narrow-laned markets, called souks. Other handicrafts include leather bags, shoes, hand-printed clothes, pottery, woven mats and baskets, brassware and carved wooden animals and masks.

♦ *South Africa produces more than half of all the continent's manufactured goods.*

INDUSTRY AND AGRICULTURE

This map shows some of the main areas where mineral resources and fossil fuels have been found, as well as agricultural areas. The most heavily industrialized mining areas are in South Africa, Zimbabwe, the Democratic Republic of Congo and Zambia. These areas have vast deposits of gold, diamonds, copper, platinum, uranium and chrome ore. Oil and natural gas are plentiful north of the Sahara, in Libya, Algeria and Egypt.

Nigeria has huge reserves of iron ore and coal, but its main export is oil.

Copper makes up 80 percent of the Democratic Republic of Congo's export industry.

Egypt extracts high-grade iron ore, which is processed into iron and steel.

Burundi has the world's richest deposits of vanadium, used to make steel alloys.

△ Diamonds
▲ Iron ore
▲ Coal
▲ Oil
△ Gold
△ Copper
△ Other minerals
○ Fruit and vegetables
○ Arable and grazing

Mining for diamonds and gold is the main activity in South Africa.

SUGAR FACTORY

Sudan, the largest country in Africa, has the biggest sugar factory on the continent and the third largest in the world, at Kanana (below). Raw sugar is made from the sweet sap of sugar cane, a giant grass that grows up to 4.5 m (15 ft) tall. It is processed into sugar crystals at the factory. Other important African crops grown for sale and export include most of the world's palm kernels, 75 percent of the world's palm oil and cocoa, and 30 percent of its high-quality cotton.

♦ *Egypt produces more dates than any other country.*

RICH IN MINERALS

Africans have mined and processed minerals, including gold, for over 2,000 years. South Africa has the richest deposits of valuable minerals. Using modern technology, today's miners are able to drill for gold and diamonds (below) very deep under ground.

♦ *The gold mine at Carletonville, South Africa, is the world's deepest mine at 3,777 m (12,392 ft).*

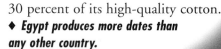

AUSTRALIA
Area: 7,682,300 sq km
Population: 18,250,000

FIJI
Area: 18,274 sq km
Population: 809,000

KIRIBATI
Area: 849 sq km
Population: 73,000

MARSHALL ISLANDS
Area: 181 sq km
Population: 45,000

MICRONESIA
Area: 702 sq km
Population: 105,000

NAURU
Area: 21 sq km
Population: 10,390

NEW ZEALAND
Area: 767,513 sq km
Population: 3,641,000

SOLOMON ISLANDS
Area: 28,370 sq km
Population: 404,000

TONGA
Area: 780 sq km
Population: 93,000

Australasia
People and places

This continent includes Australia, New Zealand and thousands of small islands scattered across the Pacific Ocean. Australia has an area over 20 times bigger than all the other countries put together, and almost three-quarters of the region's people live there. Yet most Australians live in a small part of the country, near the southeast coast. Aborigines are Australia's original inhabitants and have lived there for over 40,000 years. Maoris were the first people in New Zealand, sailing from the Polynesian islands in about AD 800. Both these peoples are now minorities in countries where the majority are descended from European settlers.

ABORIGINES

Aborigines adapted to a dry land. They learned where to find water and food, hunting with spears and boomerangs. In a dance called a corroboree (left), they celebrate their ancestral spirits.

♦ In recent years Aborigines have won back control over some of the lands that were taken from them by Europeans.

ULURU

Uluru, the Aborigines' name for Ayer's Rock, is an ancient block of sandstone in Australia's Northern Territory. It rises 348 m (1,142 ft) above the desert plain, and glows red, pink and purple in the setting sun. Uluru is a sacred place to the Aborigines. It is where many of the paths taken by their ancestral spirits meet, and there are Aboriginal paintings in the caves at the rock's base.

♦ In 1985 Uluru was returned to the local Aboriginal people, who now manage it as a national park with the Australian government.

SYDNEY HARBOUR

Sydney is Australia's oldest city. It was founded in 1788, when the first European settlers made use of its superb natural harbour. Two of the country's most famous landmarks, the Opera House and the Harbour Bridge (above), are in Sydney.

♦ The unique roofs of the Sydney Opera House, which opened in 1973, were designed to look like giant sails.

Darwin was almost completely destroyed by a cyclone on Christmas Day, 1974.

TIMOR SEA
ARAFURA SEA
INDIAN OCEAN
Melville I.
Darwin
Arnhem Land
Gulf of Carpentaria
Daly
Roper
Wyndham
Kimberley Plateau
Barkly Tableland
Derby
Fitzroy
NORTHERN TERRITORY
Georgina
Port Hedland
Great Sandy Desert
Fortescue
▲ Mt. Bruce
MACDONNELL RANGES
Tropic of Capricorn
Gibson Desert
Alice Springs
Carnarvon
▲ Uluru
Simpson Desert
Murchison
WESTERN AUSTRALIA
SOUTH AUSTRALIA
L. Eyre
Great Victoria Desert
L.Everard
L.Torrens
Kalgoorlie
Nullarbor Plain
L.Gairdner
Perth
Fremantle
Great Australian Bight
N
Adelaide
Kangaroo I.
Albany

The longest straight section of railway track in the world crosses the **Nullarbor Plain**. It is 478 km (297 mi) long!

Kilometres
0 200 400 600 800 1000

0 200 400 600
Miles

FLYING DOCTOR SERVICE

Australians in remote settlements live far away from doctors and hospitals. To deal with this problem, the Royal Flying Doctor Service was founded in 1928. With 38 aircraft, the Service provides emergency medical care across a vast area.

♦ People use radio to contact a flying doctor for medical help.

TUVALU Area: 24 sq km Population: 10,300
VANUATU Area: 14,760 sq km Population: 178,000
SAMOA Area: 2,831 sq km Population: 168,000

POLYNESIA

Many Pacific islands are the peaks of underwater mountains. Others, such as Bora Bora (right), are extinct volcanoes fringed by beautiful lagoons and coral reefs.

♦ *Bora Bora covers just 15 sq km (6 sq mi) and is home to 2,000 people. They are Polynesians who speak Tahitian.*

Data file

Area	8,041,183 sq km/3,104,725 sq mi
Population	25 million
Independent countries	12, and 9 dependencies
Largest country	Australia (7,682,300 sq km/2,966,200 sq mi)
Smallest country	Nauru (21 sq km/8 sq mi)
Most populated country	Australia (18,250,000)
Least populated country	Tuvalu (10,300)
Largest cities	Sydney, Australia (3.7 million), Melbourne, Australia (3.2 million)
Highest mountain	Mount Cook, New Zealand (3,764 m/12,316 ft)
Longest river	Murray–Darling, Australia (3,780 km/2,330 mi)
Largest lake	Eyre, Australia (9,320 sq km/3,598 sq mi)
Largest desert	Great Sandy, Australia (338,500 sq km/130,695 sq mi)
Religions	Protestant, Roman Catholic, other Christian
Languages	English, French, Maori, Samoan and native languages

How places got their names

New Zealand	after the Dutch province of Zeeland
Polynesia	from the Greek for *many islands*
Samoa	named by Maoris after the moa, a giant bird that is now extinct

Cape York

Great Dividing Range

GREAT BARRIER REEF

Cairns

Mitchell

CORAL SEA

Flinders

Townsville

SPORTING NATIONS

Australians and New Zealanders are passionate about sport. Cricket is the favourite summer game in Australia, and fans (above) flock to international games such as test matches.

♦ *The famous New Zealand rugby team is known as the All Blacks.*

Thomson

Barcoo

Belyando

Rockhampton

Fraser I.

QUEENSLAND

Brisbane

Darling

NEW SOUTH WALES

Lachlan

GREAT DIVIDING RANGE

Newcastle

PACIFIC OCEAN

Sydney

Canberra **Wollongong**

Murray AUSTRALIAN CAPITAL TERRITORY

VICTORIA ▲ *Mt. Kosciusko*

Ballarat **Melbourne**

Geelong

King I. *Bass Strait* *Flinders I.*

TASMAN SEA

Launceston

TASMANIA

Hobart

The Australian island state of **Tasmania** gets its name from the Dutch explorer, Abel Tasman, who sighted the island in 1642.

New Zealand's capital, **Wellington**, is the southernmost capital city in the world.

Auckland

North Island

Hamilton

L. Taupo

NEW ZEALAND

South Island

■ **Wellington**

SOUTHERN ALPS

Mt. Cook ▲

Christchurch

Stewart I.

MAORI MASK

Traditionally the Maoris live in tribal villages.

They still keep up their arts of tattooing and intricate wood carving, such as this mask (left).

♦ *Maoris call New Zealand Aotearoa, meaning "land of the long white cloud".*

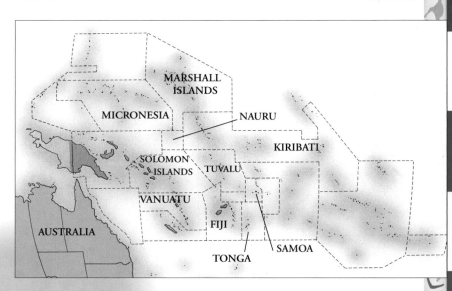

MARSHALL ISLANDS

MICRONESIA

NAURU

KIRIBATI

SOLOMON ISLANDS

TUVALU

VANUATU

FIJI

AUSTRALIA

SAMOA

TONGA

PACIFIC ISLANDS

People from South East Asia sailed to the Pacific islands in canoes about 5,000 years ago and began settling there. The islanders developed hundreds of different cultures and languages, but they all traded with each other. There are three main groups of Pacific peoples, called Polynesians, Melanesians and Micronesians. During the 19th century many of the islands became colonies of France, Britain and the United States, and the islanders converted to Christianity.

♦ *Most Pacific countries consist of many islands. Kiribati has 33 small islands, which are spread out over 3 million sq km (1.2 million sq mi) of ocean.*

71

Australasia:
Nature

Australia is an ancient land mass. It has been separated from the other continents for 65 million years. Wind, rain and sun have worked on its rocks and mountains for so long that they have worn away, making it the flattest continent. Central Australia consists of deserts of sand and stone, though the southeast is wetter. Over millions of years the region's isolation has led to the development of a number of unique species of plants and animals. Over a hundred kinds of marsupials are found in Australia. There are also unusual egg-laying mammals such as the echidna and the duck-billed platypus. New Zealand has an incredible variety of landscapes, including mountains, glaciers, hot springs, rainforests and grasslands. The country is home to unusual flightless birds such as the kiwi.

Brushtail possum

Red kangaroo

Koala

Wombat

MARSUPIALS

Female marsupials have a pouch in which their young spend their first months. Kangaroos, possums, wombats and koalas are all marsupials.

♦ *The smallest marsupial is the pygmy planigale, a tiny mouselike creature.*

FLIGHTLESS BIRDS

The largest flightless bird in Australia is the emu. New Zealand's flightless birds are smaller. The kiwi (right) is New Zealand's national bird. It has long feathers that look like fur.

♦ *The flightless takahe was thought to be extinct until it was rediscovered in 1948.*

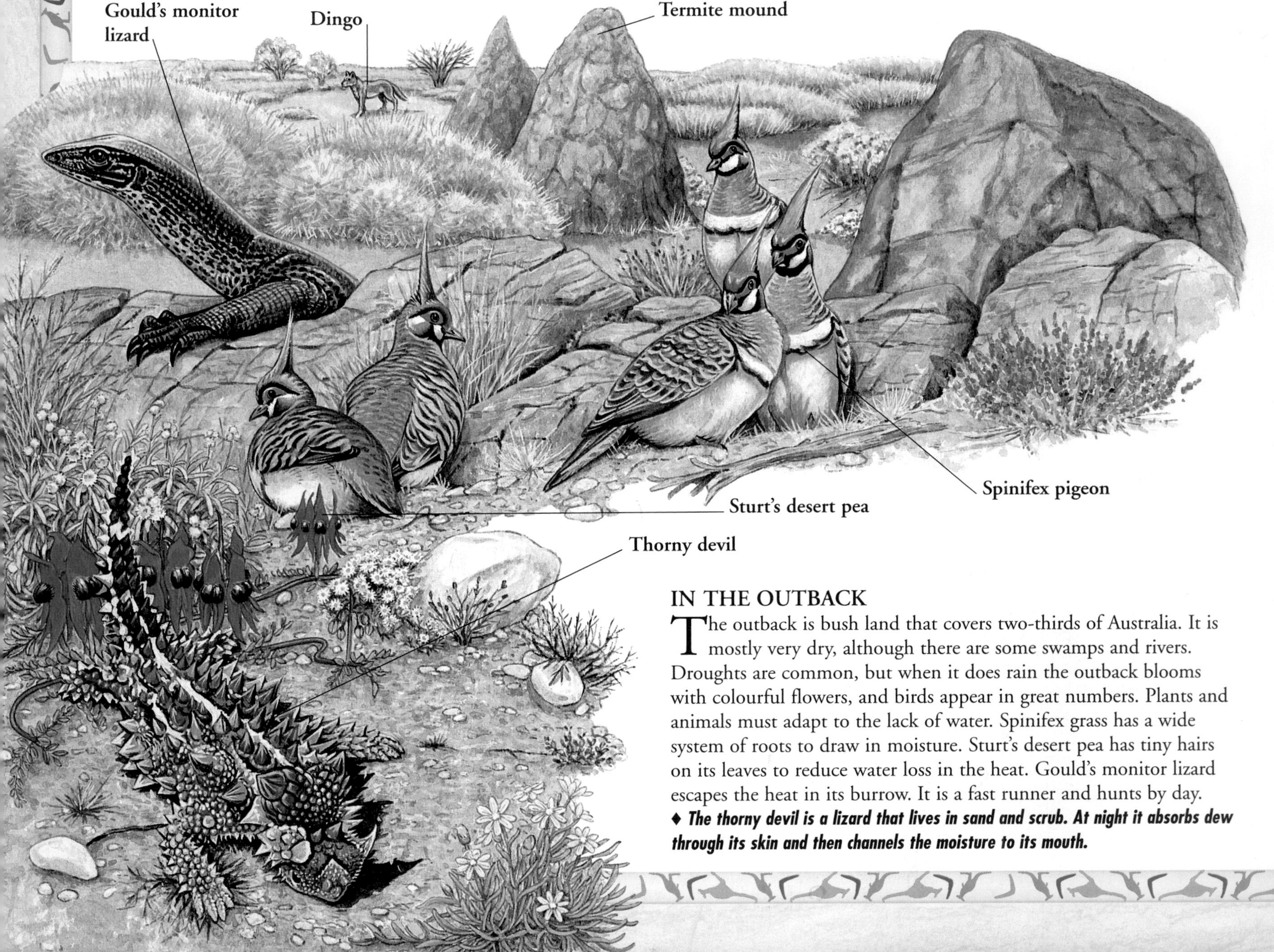

Gould's monitor lizard

Dingo

Termite mound

Spinifex pigeon

Sturt's desert pea

Thorny devil

IN THE OUTBACK

The outback is bush land that covers two-thirds of Australia. It is mostly very dry, although there are some swamps and rivers. Droughts are common, but when it does rain the outback blooms with colourful flowers, and birds appear in great numbers. Plants and animals must adapt to the lack of water. Spinifex grass has a wide system of roots to draw in moisture. Sturt's desert pea has tiny hairs on its leaves to reduce water loss in the heat. Gould's monitor lizard escapes the heat in its burrow. It is a fast runner and hunts by day.

♦ *The thorny devil is a lizard that lives in sand and scrub. At night it absorbs dew through its skin and then channels the moisture to its mouth.*

TASMANIAN WOLF

The Tasmanian wolf, or thylacine, is thought to be extinct, but every year people claim to have seen its paw marks in the remote woods of Tasmania. The wolf was a marsupial with a doglike head, and it barked and growled like a dog. It hunted at night, either alone or in pairs, feeding on wallabies, rats and birds. The last captive animal died in the 1930s.

♦ *Tasmanian wolves were hunted by humans because they attacked sheep and chickens.*

Hammerhead shark

Tiger shark

GREAT BARRIER REEF

Off the coast of northeast Australia lies the largest living structure in the world: the Great Barrier Reef. It is made up of over 2,000 individual coral reefs spread along 2,100 km (1,300 mi). Reefs are made by tiny sea creatures called coral polyps that attach themselves to rocks in huge numbers. As corals die, new ones grow on top.

♦ *Many sharks and other fish swim around the Reef.*

EUCALYPT FOREST

Eucalypts, or gum trees, were once unique to Australia. Today they are grown all over the world in gardens and commercial forests. There are hundreds of different kinds, some towering like these trees in Cathedral Range State Park, Victoria (above), and others that form small bushes.

♦ *Koalas live in gum trees and feed on the young shoots and leaves.*

Nurse shark

Spinner shark

Parrotfish

Thresher shark

Australasia: Farming and industry

TONGAN CRAFT

This woman from Tonga is painting tapa cloth, which is made from the bark of mulberry trees. Other traditional crafts on the islands are basketmaking, mat weaving and beadwork. The Tongan people are Polynesians. Most work as farmers, growing coconuts, bananas and cassava, and raising cattle, poultry and pigs. Fishing is also important.
♦ *Coconut oil is used to make soap and cosmetics.*

The wealth of Australia and New Zealand is based on farming and mining. Both countries export a great deal of farm produce, such as wool, beef, lamb and dairy products. Australia has large reserves of metals and minerals, and Australians use modern roads to get them to ports, from where they are shipped to the world's markets. The Pacific islands have far fewer natural resources, and many of the islands are so small that they have little farmland. Being so far away from the world's main centres of population makes it difficult for the islanders to export their goods. Fishing and increasing tourism help their economies.

MINING

Australia has big deposits of almost all the minerals and metals needed by a modern industrial economy. There is coal on the east coast and iron ore (left) in Western Australia. Coober Pedy, in South Australia, has the world's largest opal mine. Gold, diamonds and silver are found in other parts of the country. Many mines, such as Mount Isa in Queensland, are in harsh, dry regions, and miners work under extremely tough conditions.
♦ *The tiny island of Nauru has deposits of phosphates, used to make fertilizers. New Caledonia has valuable reserves of nickel.*

CULTURED PEARLS

French Polynesia and Australia are two of the world's leading centres of pearl farming. Pearls occur naturally inside oyster shells when a grain of sand lodges inside the shell and the oyster coats it with a hard substance called nacre. The Japanese discovered how to make so-called cultured pearls. This is done by placing a speck of oyster shell and a piece of oyster flesh inside the oyster. The oyster is then returned to the sea bed, and after about two years a pearl has formed.
♦ *Polynesia specializes in black pearls, but the most sought-after pearls are perfectly round and white.*

GEOTHERMAL POWER

The Rotorua district of New Zealand's North Island is a volcanic region steaming with hot springs, mud pools and geysers. Water beneath the Earth's surface is heated by hot volcanic rocks and rises under pressure. New Zealand has pioneered the use of this geothermal energy to produce electricity, which is used to heat homes in winter and power refrigeration units in summer. Rising steam is channelled by pipes to drive turbines. The first power plant was built at Wairakei (left). At the Ohaaki plant, water is injected back into the rocks to maintain the supply. New Zealand produces about 8 percent of its electricity this way.

♦ *At Whakarewarewa there are over 500 hot springs. Some bubble up in mud pools, and others form geysers that blast water 30 m (98 ft) into the air.*

ROAD TRAIN

In a country as vast as Australia, goods have to be taken great distances from farms and mines to markets and ports. Journeys across the outback can cover hundreds of kilometres on rough roads. Outside built-up areas, drivers sometimes attach two or three long trailers to a single truck, making a road train.

♦ *The distance from Sydney to Darwin is over 4,000 km (2,485 mi). Only one major road runs across central Australia, passing through the town of Alice Springs.*

KIWI FRUIT

New Zealand's farmers grow exotic fruits such as the Chinese gooseberry or kiwi fruit. These are grown on small farms (left).

♦ *Tamarillos, nashis and passion fruit are also grown in New Zealand.*

MODERN SYDNEY

Sydney, the state capital of New South Wales (left), is Australia's largest city, its main port and its most important manufacturing centre. Australia used to trade a lot with the United Kingdom, but since the 1970s it has done more and more business with Asia. Sydney has become the centre of Australian banking, and most of the country's largest companies have their head offices there. Many large Japanese companies also have branches in Sydney.

♦ *In Sydney you can ride by monorail from the business district to Darling Harbour, a waterfront shopping and entertainment centre.*

SHEEP FARMING

Sheep and cattle farming are big business in Australia and New Zealand. Cattle are ranched in the drier areas of Australia, but sheep need more pasture, found in wetter areas. Australian sheep farms are huge, and farmers use trucks to drive around them and feed the animals. Australia is the world's biggest exporter of wool.

♦ *After refrigerators became available in the 1880s, Australia and New Zealand were able to export meat and other foods to the rest of the world.*

HUSKY SLEDS

Before motorized snowmobiles were invented, the easiest way for people to cross the frozen Arctic wastes was by sleds pulled by huskies. These strong dogs come originally from northern Siberia. They have thick coats to keep out the cold and can pull loads up to twice their own weight. They are usually harnessed together into teams of at least six, with one husky as the lead dog. In parts of Greenland husky sleds are still the main means of transport.

♦ *Racing sleds with teams of huskies is a popular sport in parts of Alaska and northern Canada.*

The Arctic

The Arctic is the cold region around the North Pole. It consists of a large ocean — almost surrounded by land — that is always partly frozen. In winter the frozen area gets bigger and the sun barely appears above the horizon. But in summer some of the ice melts and ships can pass through. Greenland, the world's largest island, is almost entirely covered by a massive ice cap up to 3 km (1.9 mi) thick. The average temperature is -33° C (-27° F). Animals such as polar bears, hares and foxes can survive the bitter cold, and the seas are rich in fish and whales. For centuries the Inuit have lived in the Arctic, hunting and fishing.

ICEBREAKER

When the Arctic Ocean freezes in winter, ordinary ships cannot get through. Special icebreakers with reinforced hulls and very powerful engines, such as this one (left) belonging to the Russian navy, are used to crush the ice and keep the Arctic waterways open.

♦ *At the North Pole, in the centre of the Arctic region, the seas are permanently frozen.*

WHALES

Although they live in the sea, whales are mammals. They must come to the surface regularly to breathe air. Females give birth to live young and feed them with their own milk. Many different kinds of whales live in the Arctic waters, where they feed on fish and tiny sea creatures called krill. Some whales move south to warmer waters to breed.

♦ *The male Narwhal has a long, spiralling tusk up to 2.5 m (8 ft) long that it uses as a jousting weapon when competing for females.*

Narwhal

Beluga whale and calf

Humpback whale

GREENLANDERS

Most of the people of Greenland live in coastal settlements, where the ice melts for some of the year. The largest town is the capital, Godthåb (right), which has over 13,000 inhabitants. Greenlanders belong to two groups, the native Inuit and Danish settlers.

♦ *Greenland is a self-governing province of Denmark.*

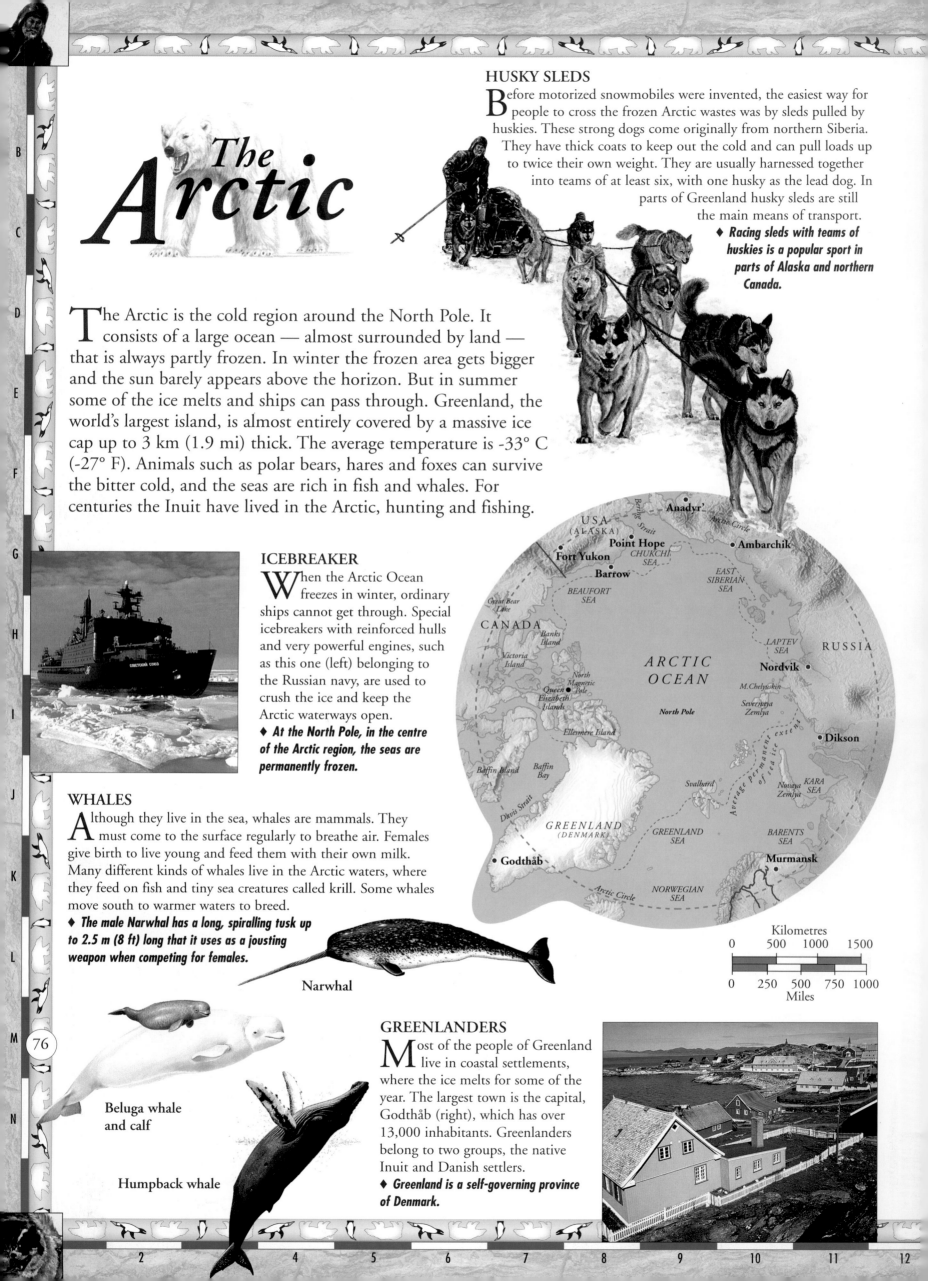

Map labels: Anadyr', USA (ALASKA), Bering Strait, Arctic Circle, Point Hope, CHUKCHI SEA, Ambarchik, Fort Yukon, Barrow, EAST SIBERIAN SEA, BEAUFORT SEA, Great Bear Lake, CANADA, Banks Island, Victoria Island, LAPTEV SEA, RUSSIA, ARCTIC OCEAN, North Magnetic Pole, Nordvik, Queen Elizabeth Islands, M. Chelyuskin, North Pole, Severnaya Zemlya, Ellesmere Island, Dikson, Baffin Island, Baffin Bay, Svalbard, Novaya Zemlya, KARA SEA, Davis Strait, GREENLAND (DENMARK), GREENLAND SEA, BARENTS SEA, Godthåb, Murmansk, Arctic Circle, NORWEGIAN SEA, Average permanent extent of sea ice

Kilometres
0   500   1000   1500

0   250   500   750   1000
Miles

Antarctica

Antarctica is the frozen continent that surrounds the South Pole. A giant ice cap covers the land. Beneath the ice lie mountains and valleys. In winter temperatures drop to -50° C (-58° F) and fierce winds blow from the high ground. In 1911 the Norwegian explorer Roald Amundsen and his team became the first people to reach the South Pole.

ICEBERGS

Icebergs occur in both the Arctic and Antarctic regions. They form when huge chunks of ice break off from ice sheets or glaciers that meet the sea. Ocean currents can move them great distances into warmer water, where they can be a hazard to shipping.

♦ **Over 90 percent of an iceberg's mass is below the ocean's surface.**

PENGUINS

Penguins are found widely along the coasts of Antarctica and in the surrounding waters of the Southern Ocean. These gentoo penguins (right) nest in huge colonies called rookeries on the Antarctic peninsula and South Georgia. They make nests from stones and grass, and lay two eggs. For a month the parents take turns to incubate the eggs. When the chicks hatch, they huddle together for safety from predators.

♦ **Emperor penguins, the largest species, can be up to 1 m (3 ft) tall.**

LICHENS

Lichens (left) grow where no other living things can survive, including high on Antarctic mountains. They cling to bare rock surfaces, growing by tiny amounts each year. Some lichens can live for 4,000 years.

♦ **Lichens are living partnerships between fungi and algae.**

Map labels

ATLANTIC OCEAN
INDIAN OCEAN
S. Orkney Is
C. Norvegia
Average permanent extent of sea ice
Antarctic Circle
S. Shetland Is
WEDDELL SEA
Dronning Maud Land
Enderby Land
Coats Land
Graham Land
Antarctic Peninsula
Palmer Land
Palmer Archipelago
Mac Robertson Land
Alexander I.
Berkner I.
Ronne Ice Shelf
PENSACOLA MTNS.
CHARLES MTNS
Amery Ice Shelf
Charcot I.
BELLINGHAUSEN SEA
Ellsworth Land
Vinson Massif
South Pole
GREATER ANTARCTICA
Peter I.
Mt. Seelig
TRANSANTARCTIC MOUNTAINS
Queen Mary Land
Shackleton Ice Shelf
Thurston I.
LESSER ANTARCTICA
QUEEN MAUD MTNS.
Knox Coast
AMUNDSEN SEA
Mt. Kirkpatrick
Wilkes Land
Siple I.
Marie Byrd Land
Mt. Markham
Ross Ice Shelf
C. Poinsett
Mt. Sidley
Roosevelt I.
Victoria Land
PACIFIC OCEAN
C. Colbeck
ROSS SEA
Terre Adélie
Dates Land
George V Land
South Magnetic Pole
Antarctic Circle
C. Adare
Scott I.
Sturge I.

Scale

Kilometres
0 500 1000 1500

0 250 500 750 1000
Miles

AMUNDSEN-SCOTT STATION

No one lives permanently in Antarctica, but many countries have scientific bases there. The American Amundsen-Scott station (below) lies at the South Pole. Scientists at the bases extract ice samples from deep inside the ice cap to investigate how the Earth's climate has changed over thousands of years.

♦ **British explorer Robert Scott was second to reach the South Pole. He died on the way back.**

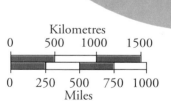

Data file

Area of the Arctic Ocean	13,230,000 sq km/5,108,000 sq mi
Area of Antarctica	14,245,000 sq km/5,500,000 sq mi
Highest mountain	Vinson Massif, Antarctica (5,140 m/16,863 ft)
Longest glacier	Lambert Glacier, Antarctica (700 km/435 mi)
Largest lake	Great Bear, Arctic Canada (31,328 sq km/ 12,096 sq mi)
Countries above the Arctic Circle	Greenland (Denmark), Canada, USA (Alaska), Russia, Finland, Sweden, Norway
Countries with bases in Antarctica	USA, Russia, United Kingdom, Argentina, Australia, Chile, France, India, New Zealand

How places got their names

Antarctica	means opposite the Arctic
Arctic	from the Greek for *bear* and the Great Bear constellation
Greenland	named by the Vikings, who found grass near the shore

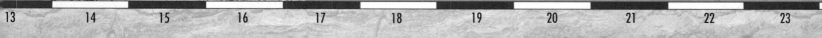

Index and Gazetteer

In this index and gazetteer, page numbers refer to a text entry in the book. If the page number is prefixed by ✎, there is also a picture of the subject. Places shown on the maps have a page number followed by a grid reference (e.g. **Banks Island** 76 H7). Turn to the page (76), then use your finger to trace a line from the letter (H) across the page. Trace another line from the number (7) up the page. Where the two points meet, you will find the place on the map.

Abbreviations of countries controlling dependencies:

DENMARK	Denmark
FR	France
ECUADOR	Ecuador
INDIA	India
NETH	Netherlands
NZ	New Zealand
PORT	Portugal
SPAIN	Spain
UK	United Kingdom
US	United States of America

Aa

Abadan Iran 45 I14
Abidjan Ivory Coast 64 H-I8
Abilene, Kansas USA 15 H13, 19
Abilene, Texas USA 14 J12
Aborigines, Australian ✎70
Abu Dhabi United Arab Emirates 45 J16
Abuja Nigeria 64 H9-10
Ab ukuma Japan 63 I14
Acapulco Mexico 20 I9
Accra Ghana 64 H-I8
Aconcagua, Mount Argentina 24 K8, 25
Adana Turkey 44 F10
Ad Dahna Saudi Arabia 45 I13
Addis Ababa Ethiopia 65 H14
Adelaide Australia 70 K12
Aden Yemen 45 N13
Adriatic Sea 35 I13, 36
Aegean Sea 35 K16, 36
Afghanistan 42, 48, 48 E10, 52, 53
Agra India ✎49, 49 G-H14
Aguascalientes Mexico 20 G8
Ahaggar Algeria 64 F9
Ahmadabad India 48 H12
Ajmer India 49 H13
Akita Japan 63 G14
Aksu China 58 F10
Alabama River 15 J16
Åland 31 H16
Alaska USA 10 F7, 14, 14 A10, 16, 18, 76 G8, 77
Albania 34, 35 J15
Albany Australia 70 K8
Albany, Georgia USA 15 J16
Albany, New York USA 15 H18
Albuquerque USA 14 I10
Aldanskoye Nagor'ye Russia 41 H-I16
Aleutian Islands 14 B9
Alexandria Egypt 65 E13
Algeria 64, 64 E9, 68
Algiers Algeria 64 D9
Al Hudaydah Yemen 44 N12
Alice Springs Australia 70 H11
Al Jawf Saudi Arabia 44 I11
Allahabad India 49 H15
alligator ✎16
Alma-Ata Kazakhstan 40 L10
Al Manamah Bahrain 45 J15
Al Mukalla Yemen 45 N14
Alps Europe 34 H11, 35, 36, 39
Altai Mountains Mongolia 59 E13
Altiplano Bolivia 24 I8
Altun Shan China 58 G12
Amazon River Brazil 8 I11, 24 F10, 25, 26
Ambarchik Russia 76 G10
Amderma Russia 40 G10
Amman Jordan 44 H10
Amritsar India ✎48
Amsterdam Netherlands 34 E11
Amu Dar'ya River Turkmenistan 40 M8
Amundsen Sea Antarctica 77 I14
Anadyr' Russia 41 E18, 76 F9
Andalusia Spain ✎39
Andaman Islands 49 M17, 53
Andes Mountains 24, 24 G6, ✎25, ✎26, 29
Andorra la Vella Andorra 34 I9
Andros Island Bahamas 21 F15
Angara River Russia 41 I13
Angkor Wat Cambodia ✎54
Angola 64, 64 K11
Anguilla 21 F-G19
Ankara Turkey 44 E9
Annaba Algeria 64 D10
An Nafud Saudi Arabia 44 I11
Annapolis USA 15 H18
Annapurna, Mount Nepal 49 G15
An Nasiriyah Iraq 45 H13
Antarctica ✎77, 77 I17
Antigua and Barbuda 20, 21 G19
Antofagasta Chile 24 J8
Aomori Japan 63 F14
Apennines Italy 35 J13, 37
Appalachian Mountains USA 15 I16, 16
Arabian Desert 45
Arabian Sea 45 M17
Arafura Sea 70 E11
Araguaia River Brazil 24 G11
Aral Sea Kazakhstan/Uzbekistan 40 K8, ✎42, 43
Arctic 32, 42, ✎76, 77
Arctic fox ✎13
Arctic hare 13
Arctic Ocean 31 C17, 41 E13, ✎76, 76 H9, 77
argali ✎60
Argentina ✎24, 24 K9, 26, 28, 77
Århus Denmark 31 J14
Arica Chile 24 I8
Arinos River Brazil 24 G10
Arizona USA ✎16, 17
Arkansas River USA 14 I12, 15 I14
Arkhangel'sk Russia 40, 40 G8
Armenia 44, 45 E13
Arnhem Land Australia 70 F11
Aruba 21 I17
Asahi dake Japan 63 C15
Asahikawa Japan 63 C15
Ashkhabad Turkmenistan 40 M7
Asia, Southern ✎48, ✎49, ✎50, ✎51, ✎52, ✎53
  South East ✎54, ✎55, ✎56, ✎57
  South West ✎44, ✎45, ✎46, ✎47
Asir Saudi Arabia 44 L12
Asmera Eritrea 65 G14
ass ✎60
Assam India 53
Assyrians 46
Astana Kazakhstan 40 K10
Astrakhan Russia 40 J7
Asunción Paraguay 24 J10
Aswan Egypt 65 F13
Asyut Egypt 65 F13
Atacama Desert Chile 24 I8, ✎26
Atbara Sudan 65 G13-14
Athabasca River Canada 10 I11
Athens Greece 35 K16
Atlanta USA 15 J16
Atlantic Ocean 15 J18, 24 E13, 33
Atlas Mountains Morocco 64 E8
Auckland New Zealand 71 L20
Augusta, Georgia USA 15 J17
Augusta, Maine USA 15 F19
Austin USA 15 K13
Australia/Australasia ✎70, 70 H11, ✎71, ✎72, ✎73, ✎74, ✎75, 77
Austria 34, 35 H13
Ayer's Rock (Uluru) Australia ✎70, 70 I10
Azerbaijan 45 E14, 45 F13
Aztec people 20

Bb

Babol Iran 45 F15
Babylon 46
badger ✎33
Baffin Bay 11 E14, 76 J7
Baffin Island Canada 8 E-F11, 9, 11, 11 E14, 76 I-J7
Baghdad Iraq 45, 45 H13
Bahamas 21 E15
Bahawalpur Pakistan 48 F-G12
Bahía Blanca Argentina 24 L9
Bahrain 44, 45, 45 J15, 46
Baikal, Lake Russia 41 J14, ✎43
Baikonur Kazakhstan 40, 40 K9
Baja California 20 E5
Bakersfield USA 14 I7
Baku Azerbaijan 45 E14
Balaton, Lake Hungary 35, 35 H14, 37
Balearic Islands 34 J9
Bali Indonesia 54 L10, ✎55, ✎57
Balikpapan Borneo 54 K10
Balkan Peninsula 36
Balkhash Kazakhstan 40 L10
Balkhash, Lake Kazakhstan 40 L10
Ballarat Australia 71 K13
Balsas River Mexico 20 H-I9
Baltic Sea 31 J16, 36
Baltic states 30
Baltimore USA 15 G-H18
Bamako Mali 64 G7
Bandar Abbas Iran 45 I16
Bandar e Lengeh Iran 45 J16
Bandar Seri Begawan Brunei 54 I-J10
Banda Sea 55 K13
Bandung Java 54 L8
Bangalore India 49 L13, ✎53
Bangkok Thailand 54, 54 H6-7, 55
Bangladesh 48, 49 I17, 51, ✎52, 53
Bangor USA 15 E19
Bangui Central African Republic 64 I11
Banjarmasin Borneo 54 K10
Banjul Gambia 64 G6
Banks Island Canada 10 E11, 76 H7
Baotou China 59 F16
Barbados 21 H20
Barcelona Spain 34 I9
Barcoo River Australia 71 H14
Barents Sea 40 F9, 76 J10
Barkly Tableland Australia 70 G11
Barragem de Sobradinho Brazil 25 G13
Barranquilla Colombia 24 D7
Barrow USA 14 A11, 76 G8
Bass Strait 71 L14
Baton Rouge USA 15 K14
bats ✎23, ✎27
Batumi Georgia 40 K5
Bayan Har Shan China 59 H14
Bay of Bengal 49 J17
Bay of Biscay 34 H8
Bay of Campeche 20 H10
Bay of Fundy Canada 11 J18
bears ✎12, 16, 37
Beaufort Sea 10 E10, 76 G8
beaver 12, ✎16-17, 35
Bedouin people ✎44
Beijing China 59 F17
Beira Mozambique 65 L13
Beirut Lebanon 44 G10
Belarus 40, 40 G-H6
Belém Brazil 24 F12
Belfast Northern Ireland 30 J9
Belgium 34, 34 F11
Belgrade Yugoslavia 35 I15
Belize 20, 20 I12
Belize City Belize 20 H12
Bellinghausen Sea Antarctica 77 I14
Belmopan Belize 20 H12
Belo Horizonte Brazil 24 I12
Belyando River Australia 71 H14
Bend USA 14 F7
Bengal, Bay of 49
Bengal India 53
Benghazi Libya 64 E12
Benin 64, 64 H9, 65
Benue River Nigeria 64 H10
Berbera Somalia 65 H15
Bergen Norway 31 H13
Bering Sea 10 F5, 14 A9, 41 D18
Bering Strait 41 C17, 76 F8
Berlin Germany 34, 35 F13
Bern Switzerland 34 H11
Bhavnagar India 48 I11
Bhutan 48, 49, 49 H17, 52
Bialowieza National Park Poland 35
Bihar India 53
Bilbao Spain 34 H8
birds of paradise ✎56
Birmingham England 30 K10
Birmingham USA 15 J16
Bishkek Kyrgyzstan 40 L10
Bismarck USA 14 F12
bison ✎16, 17, 35
Bissau Guinea Bissau 64 G-H6
Biwa, Lake Japan 62 K11, 63
blackbird ✎33
Black Sea 35 I18, 39, 44 D9
Blantyre Malawi 65 L14
Blue Nile River Africa 65 H14
Blue Ridge Mountains USA 17
bobolink ✎17
Bogotá Colombia 24 E7, 25
Bo Hai China 59 F18
Boise USA 14 G8
Bolivia ✎24, 24 H9, 29
Bombay (Mumbai) India 48, 48 J11-12, 49, ✎52
Bora Bora Polynesia ✎71
Bordeaux France 34 H9
Borneo 9, 54 K10, 56
Bosnia-Herzegovina 35, 35 I14
Bosporus Strait 44
Boston USA 15 F19
Botswana 64, 64 L12
Bougainville 55 H18-19
Boulder USA 14 H11
Brahmaputra River India/ Bangladesh 49, 49 H18, 51
Branco River Brazil 24 E9
Brasília Brazil 24 H11, 25
Bratislava Slovakia 35 G14
Bratsk Russia 41 J13
Brazzaville Congo 64 J11
Brazil 9, 24, 24 G9, ✎25, ✎26, ✎27, ✎28, ✎29
Brazilian Highlands Brazil 24 I12
Brazos River USA 14 J12
Brisbane Australia 71 I16
British Columbia Canada 13
Brittany France ✎34
Bruce, Mount Australia 70 H7
Brunei 54, 54 J10
Brussels Belgium 34 F11
Bucharest Romania 35 I16-17
Budapest Hungary 35 H14-15
Buenos Aires Argentina 8, 8 J11, ✎24, 24 K10, 25
Buffalo USA 15 G17
Bug River Poland 35 F15
Bujumbura Burundi 65 J13
Bukhara Uzbekistan 40 M8
Bulawayo Zimbabwe 65 L13
Bulgaria 34, 35 I16
Bungo Channel Japan 62 L8
Buraydah Saudi Arabia 45 J13
Burkina Faso 64, 64 H8
Burundi 64, 65 J13, 69
Bushehr Iran 45 I15
bustard, great ✎42
butterflies ✎37

Cc

Cagliari Sardinia 34 K11
Cairns Australia 71 F14
Cairo Egypt ✎65, 65 E13
Calcutta India 49, 49 I17
Calgary Canada 10 J10, ✎11
Cali Colombia 24 E6
California USA 16, 17, 18
Camagüey Cuba 21 G15
Camargue France ✎36, 37
Cambodia ✎54, 55
camels ✎44, ✎51, ✎59, ✎65
Cameroon 64, 64 I10
Campeche Mexico 20 H12
Campos Brazil 24 I12
Canada 9, ✎10, 10 H4, ✎11, ✎12, ✎13, 76, 77
Canadian River USA 14 I12
Canary Islands 64 E7
Canberra Australia 71 K14-15
Cantabrian Mountains Spain 37
Cape Canaveral USA 15 K17
Cape Cod USA 15 F19
Cape Comorin India 48 N12
Cape Horn 24, 24 O9
Cape of Good Hope 64, 64 N11
Cape Town South Africa 64 N11
Cape York Australia 71 E13
Caracas Venezuela 24 D8
Cardiff Wales 30 L9
Caribbean Sea 20, 21 I15,✎22, ✎23, 24 C7
caribou ✎12
Carnarvon Australia 70 I6
Carpathian Mountains 35 H17, 36, 37
Carson City USA 14 H7
Casablanca Morocco 64 E8
Cascade Range USA 14 F7
Caspian Sea 8, 9, 9 G15, 40 K6-7, 42, 43, 45, 45 F15
Caucasus Mountains 40, 40 J6
Cauca Valley Colombia 29
Cayenne French Guiana 24 E11
Cayman Islands 21 H14
Celebes Sea 54 I12
Central African Republic 64, 64 H11-12
Central America 20, ✎22, ✎23
Cerro Aconcagua Argentina 24 K8
Chad 64 G11, 65
Chad, Lake 64 H11
Changchun China 59 D18, ✎60
Chang Jiang (Yangtze) River China 8, 9 H17, 59, 59 H16
Changsha China 59 H17
Chari River Chad 64 H11
Charleston, South Carolina USA 15 J17
Charleston, West Virginia USA 15 H17
Charlotte USA 15 I17
Charlottetown Canada 11 J18
cheetahs 67
Chelyabinsk Russia 40 J9
Chelyuskin Russia 76 I10
Chengdu China 59 H15
Cherskogo Range Russia 41 G16
Chesapeake Bay 15 H18
Cheyenne USA 14 H11
Chiba Japan 63 J14
Chicago USA 15 G15, ✎19
Chihuahua Mexico 20 E7-8
Chile 24, 24 J8, 25, ✎26, ✎29, 77
Chimborazo Ecuador 24 F6
China 9, 50, ✎58, ✎59, 59 H15, ✎60, ✎61
chinook 13
Chittagong Bangladesh 49 I18, ✎52
Chongqing China 59 I16
Christchurch New Zealand 71 M19
Chubut River Argentina 24 M9
Chukchi Sea 76 G9
Chuquicamata Chile ✎29
Churchill Canada 11 I13
Cimarron River USA 14 I12
Cincinnati USA 15 H16
Ciudad Juárez Mexico 20 E7
Cleveland USA 15 G16
coal 18, 42, 69
Coatzacoalcos Mexico 20 H11
Cochin India 48 M12
Coimbatore India 48 M12
Colombia 24, 24 E7, 25, 26, 28, 29
Colombo Sri Lanka 49 O13
Colorado plateau USA ✎16
Colorado River Argentina 24 L8
Colorado River USA 14 I8
Colorado Springs USA 14 H11
Columbia USA 15 I17
Columbia River USA 14 F7
Columbus USA 15 H16
Conakry Guinea 64 H6
Concord USA 15 F19
Congo 64 I-J11, 65
Congo, Democratic Republic of 64 I12, 65, 68, 69
Congo River Africa 64 I12, 67
Cook, Mount New Zealand 71, 71 M18
Copenhagen Denmark 31 K14
copper ✎29, 68, 69
coral reefs 66, 73
Coral Sea 71 G15
Córdoba Argentina 24 K9
Cork Republic of Ireland 30 K8
cormorants ✎33, ✎60
Corsica 34 I11
Costa Rica 20, 21 J13, 23
cougar ✎17
Crete 35 L16
Croatia 34, 35 H14
crocodiles ✎67
Cuba 20, 21 G14
Cubango River Angola 64 K11
Culiacán Mexico 20 F7
Cuttack India 49 J16
Cyprus 44, 44 G9, 45
Czech Republic 34, ✎35, 35 G13

Dd

Daba Shan China 59 H16
Dagupan Philippines 54 G11
Dakar Senegal 64 G6
Dalian China 59 E18
Dallas USA 15 J13
Dalou Shan China 59 I16
Daly River Australia 70 F10
Damascus Syria 44 G-H10
Damavand, Mount Iran 45, 45 G15
Da Nang Vietnam 54 H8
Danube River Europe 34 G12, 35, 35 I16, 37, 39
Dar-es-Salaam Tanzania 65 J14
Darjiling India 53
Darling River Australia 71 J13
Darwin Australia 70, 70 E-F10
Dasht-e-kavir Iran 45 G16
Dasht-e-Lut Iran 45 H17
Daugava River Latvia 31 J18
Davao Philippines 54 H12
Davenport USA 15 G14
Davis Strait 76 J7
Dayton USA 15 H16
Deccan India 49, 49 J13
deer ✎33, ✎42, ✎51, ✎61
Delphi Greece ✎34
Denmark 30, 31, 31 K13, 33
Denver USA 14 H11
Derby Australia 70 G8
Des Moines USA 15 G14
Desna River Ukraine 35 F18
Detroit USA 15 G16, 19
Dhaka Bangladesh 48, 49 I17
Diamantina River Australia 71 H13
diamonds 68, 69, 74
Dikson Russia 40 G12, 76 I11
Dili Timor 55 L13
dingo ✎72
Diyarbakir Turkey 44 F11
Djakarta Indonesia 54, 54 L8, 55
Djibouti Somalia 65 H15
Dneiper River Ukraine 35 G19
Dniester River Ukraine 35 G17
Dodoma Tanzania 65 J14
Dogo Japan 62 J9
Doha Qatar 45 J15
Dominica 20, 21 G19-20
Dominican Republic 20, 21 G17
Doñana National Park Spain 37
Donetsk Ukraine 35 G19
Dongting, Lake China 59 H17
Don River Russia 40 I6
dormouse ✎37
Dover USA 15 G18
Dozen Japan 62 J9
Drakensburg Mountains South Africa 64 N12
Dubai United Arab Emirates 45 J16
Dublin Republic of Ireland 30 K9
Duero River Spain 34 I7
Duluth USA 15 F14
dung beetle ✎46
Durango Mexico 20 G8
Durban South Africa 65 M13
Dushanbe Tajikistan 40 M9
Düsseldorf Germany 34 F11
Dzhugdzhur Range Russia 41 H17

Ee

eagles ✎22, ✎37
East China Sea 59 H19
Eastern Ghats India 49 K14
East Siberian Sea 41 E16, 76 G10
Ebro River Spain 34 I8
Ecuador 24, 24 F6
Edinburgh Scotland 30 J10
Edmonton Canada 10 I10
Egypt ✎64, 65 F13, ✎65, 68, 69
El Aaiun Western Sahara 64 E-F7
Elba 34 I12
Elbe River Germany 35 E13
Elbert, Mount USA 14 H10-11
Elburz Mountains Iran 45 G15
elephant 50, ✎53, ✎66, 67
Ellesmere Island Canada 11 D13, 76 I8
El Obeid Sudan 65 H13
El Paso USA 14 J10
El Salvador 20, 20 I-J12
Empty Quarter (Rub'al Khali) Saudi Arabia 45, 45 L14, 47
emu 72
England 30 K-L10
English Channel 30 L10
Equatorial Guinea 64 I10, 65
Erie, Lake Canada/USA 11 K15, 15 G16
Eritrea 65, 65 G14
Esfahan Iran 45 H15
Espanola Galápagos Islands ✎26
Estonia 30, 31 I17-18, 32
Ethiopia 65, 65 H14
Eugene USA 14 F7
Euphrates River Syria/Iraq 44, 44 G11, 45
Europe
  East, West and South ✎34, ✎35, ✎36, ✎37, ✎38, ✎39
  Northern ✎30, ✎31, ✎32, ✎33
Everard, Lake Australia 70 J11
Everest, Mount Nepal/China 8, 9 H16, 49, 49 G16, ✎50, 58 I11, 59
Everglades USA 15 L17, 16
Eyre, Lake Australia 70 I12

Ff

Faeroe Islands ✎30, 30 F-G10
Fairbanks USA 14 A11
Faisalabad Pakistan 48 F12
Falkland Islands 24, 24 N10, 27
Fargo USA 15 F13
F'Dérik Mauritania 64 F7
Fernandina Galápagos Islands ✎26
Fiji 71 J21-22
Finland 30, 31 G17, 32, 77
Fitzroy River Australia 70 G8
flamingoes ✎36, 67
Flinders Island Australia 71 L14
Flinders River Australia 71 G13
Flores 54 L12
Florida USA 16, ✎18
Florida Keys USA 15 L17-18
forest pigs 66
Fortaleza Brazil 25 F13
Fortescue River Australia 70 H7
Fort McPherson Canada 10 F9
Fort Norman Canada 10 G10
Fort Worth USA 15 J13
Fort Yukon USA 76 G7
foxes ✎33
France ✎34, 34 G10, 35, ✎36, 37, 38, 39, 77
Frankfort USA 15 H16
Frankfurt Germany 34 F12
Franz Josef Land 40 E11
Fraser Island Australia 71 H-I16
Fredericton Canada 11 J17
Freetown Sierra Leone 64 H6-7
Fremantle Australia 70 J7
French Guiana 24 E11
frigate bird ✎26
Fuji, Mount Japan 63, 63 J13
Fuji River Japan 63 J-K13
Fukui Japan 62 J11
Fukuoka Japan 62 L7
Fukushima Japan 63 H14
Fuzhou China 59 I19

Gg

Gabon 64 I10, 66
Gaborone Botswana 64 M12
Gairdner, Lake Australia 70 J11-12
Galápagos Islands ✎26
Galle Sri Lanka 49 O13
Galveston USA 15 K13-14
Gambia 64 G6, ✎65, 66
Ganges River India/Bangladesh 48, 49, 49 H15, 51, 53
gannets ✎32, 33
Garonne River France 34 H9
Gauhati India 49 H18
gazelles ✎60
Geelong Australia 71 L13
Genghis Khan 59
Georgetown Guyana 24 D10
Georgia 40, 40 K6
Georgina River Australia 70 G12

79